Oil for the Wounded

Dr. Charlotte Russell Johnson

Author of

A Journey to Hell & Back

This Wound

This wound went deep inside...
It was too deep to hide...
Although I tried and tried,
So many times I cried...

This wound became my banner of pride....
It was too precious to hide...
It was to me that I lied...
It kept leaking outside...

It wasn't just an injury...
It carried fury...
Forgiveness was blurry...
My pain would convince any jury...

It burned from within...
Pride was its friend...
Why should I bend?
Where would I begin?

It had lasted too long...
How could it ever be gone?
I had a reason to moan...
Many times I would groan...

This pain clouded my identity...
It threatened to rob me of all dignity...
It was a different trinity...
Gloom, misery, and disparity...

It didn't bump or rub against me...
It didn't brush lightly against me...
With sharpness, it tore into me...
My heart, it ripped from me...

I heard a song from afar...
"Is your all on the altar?"
Had I given Him my body and soul?
Had I allowed Him to take control?

I was the traveler wounded on the road...
Many refused to help lighten my load...
One day, a merciful stranger passed by...
He heard the moaning of my cry...

With unselfish love,
He extended a hand from above...
He appeared as a dove...
What sacrificial love...

There was oil in His hand...
It was good for the ailments of man...

My healing was His plan...
He wanted to help me stand...

He understood my wound...
It had led Him to a tomb...
Oh, the depth of His wound...
Many thought it would be His doom...

With a slight tilt of His hand,
My wish became His command...
Oil began to cover this man ...
My death was not at hand...

With each drop of oil,
It purified the soil...
It wrapped my wound with a coil...
The plan of an enemy, it did spoil...

The wound is no longer there...
Because a stranger took time to care...
My burdens He chose to bear...
When no one would even dare...

In Memory

Of

Helen Turner

"Mama T"

FEBRUARY 29, 1932 – JANUARY 8, 2012

INSIDE THE WOUNDS

Preface...9

Introduction...13

Hurt or Wounded..17

Salty Wounds..25

Wounds Reopened..29

Lost in Black and White...........................37

The Sacred Pulpit...41

For Your Glory...47

Proper Reproof...51

Godly Correction..63

If Virtuous Loses Virtue..........................85

Oil for the Divorced....................................93

God and God Alone.......................................97

Oil for the Married...................................103

Prelude to a Drama…………………..105

I do Love U!.……………………..…….125

Touching and Agreeing………………..135

The Letter……………………..…..…157

Sin and Slander…………………..….167

Maintaining Integrity………………..…..177

Use for the Useless……………………183

Self-Inflicted……………………..…...191

Wilt Thou………………………………197

God Made Me……………………..…….203

Appendix……………………….…..227

Preface

One day, a friend called to share her concerns with me. She was concerned about a conversation that had taken place between her and a special friend. As she shared, I listened. She shared a conversation that had been repeated between them on numerous occasions. She said that he was holding on to his painful memories.

His scales are his pride,
shut up together as with a close seal.
Job 41:15

After she finished relating the information, she asked me why he seemed so proud of his pain. It appears that his pain has almost become a badge of honor. Immediately I responded, "He's not hurt; he's wounded." Confused, she responded, "What's the difference?" Although I had never thought about this difference, from within me the answer began to come. After listening to my explanation, she asked, "How do I help him to heal?" I didn't have an answer. Looking for a solution, she asked her question a second time. This time, God gave me the answer, "You have to pour oil into the wound." That was the birth of this book, *Oil for the Wounded.*

Each of my books has a unique message of hope. The first book, *A Journey to Hell and Back* was an autobiographical account of my life. It details major events in my life, which almost destroyed me. These events were shared to provide hope and encouragement to others who have been beaten by the trials of life.

My second book, *Daddy's Hugs* exhorts the role of fathers in the lives of children. The book praises and provides examples of fathers who take a diligent role in parenting. It also shared my appreciation for several men in my life who have been positive male role models.

My third book, *A Journey to Hell and Back: The Flip Side* tells both sides of the journey. *The Flip Side* is my husband, Henry's version of the events in our lives. We shared our separate struggles, which became a common struggle. The book focused on our different past experiences that influenced our future.

In *Grace Under Fire*, I discussed unfavorable or controversial issues to the body of Christ. My husband was portrayed very accurately, although sometimes unflatteringly. The purpose of the book wasn't flattery. Actually, it discussed the dangers of a flattering woman.

Mama May I is my fifth book. It explores

the extensive effects of substance abuse and its effects on the family system. My eighth book, *Kissin' Hell Goodbye* picked up where *Mama May I* ended.

Mama's Pearls is my sixth book. It relates many words of wisdom that my mother has shared with me. It is a tribute to the woman who prayed me out of hell. The book is humorous at times.

My seventh book, *Breaking the Curse* further explores family dysfunctions and secrets. It challenges each of us to face hidden demons in our families. We are encouraged to take a stand for the littlest victims.

Kissin' Hell Goodbye is the eighth book in my series of inspirational texts. Rather than simply describing the emotions of my characters, I used the poetry in songs to convey their feelings and inner turmoil, specific plot points, and to weave together the entire drama. This is a very pithy way of providing the reader knowledge about the character's feelings while invoking an emotional response from them based on their own past experiences with the songs in the book.

All scripture references are from the King James Bible unless otherwise noted.

For more information on Religious Extremism go to www.watchman.org/cults/death.htm

For Those Tears I Died

Written by Marsha Stevens

You said You'd be there for all my tomorrows;
I came so close to sending You away,
But just like You promised You came there to stay;
I just had to pray!

And Jesus said, "Come to the water, stand by My side,
I know you are thirsty, you won't be denied;
I felt ev'ry teardrop when in darkness you cried,
And I strove to remind you that for those tears I died."

Your goodness so great I can't understand,
And, dear Lord, I know that all this was planned;
I know You're here now, and always will be,
Your love loosed my chains and in You I'm free;
But Jesus, why me?

And Jesus said, "Come to the water, stand by My side,
I know you are thirsty, you won't be denied;
I felt ev'ry teardrop when in darkness you cried,
And I strove to remind you that for those tears I died."

Jesus, I give You my heart and my soul,
I know that without God I'd never be whole;
Savior, You opened all the right doors,
I thank You and praise You from earth's humble shores;
Take me, I'm Yours.

And Jesus said, "Come to the water, stand by My side,
I know you are thirsty, you won't be denied;
I felt ev'ry teardrop when in darkness you cried,
And I strove to remind you that for those tears I died."

Introduction by Earline Hall

Oil for the Wounded is the ninth book in author Charlotte Johnson's series of motivational text. Dr. Johnson is able to use the metaphor of a wound and a hurt to clarify the harm of unresolved emotional crisis leaving deep permeating scars in the life of the injured. While pain and suffering is a part of the human existence, Dr. Johnson is able to move the reader and those connected to her to a place of acceptance and healing. Pain is unavoidable but it does not have to be the end of the story, crippling and debilitating the wounded. Dr. Johnson is able to provide a fresh, entertaining, and refreshing take on what could be a very heavy issue to address. She is able to keep the reader intrigued and laughing so that in the end, they have been educated, helped, empowered and most of all amused by her charming wit and use of anecdotal tales of her family, friends, and associates.

The book presents help for recovery in colloquial, non-medical and non-clinical ways reminiscent of the Chicken Soup for the Soul series. It differs in that it is applicable to adaptation into a professional treatment environment.

The level of transparency in this novel has eclipsed the others in this series, which seems impossible, given the very candid nature in which Dr. Johnson has unfolded her life story to the world. One of the most notorious characters in the series, Dr. Johnson's first husband reappears following a five book absence from the series. His long-awaited return answers many of the questions that loyal followers of the series have had about his fate. Although Dr. Johnson has always encouraged her fans not to harbor bitterness of resentment against him, it was difficult for her most devout fans to understand how they were able to maintain a friendship following A Journey to Hell and Back. His character is every bit as complex as Dan Scott in the popular American television series One Tree Hill. An individual capable of diverse and complicated motives and actions, he has always remained devoted to his son although his expression of love is not in a typical manner. He struggled to maintain a connection with his children despite his inappropriate choices.

Joe, much like Nathan Scott in OTH, had a different experience and relationship with his father than the siblings who were not in consistent contact with him. As Dan Scott exited the series if not redeemed, he was a more humane and likable character; Oil for the Wounded offers the same in-depth analysis into the complexity of Dr. Johnson's first husband and his efforts to move forward with his family connections although he is not able to completely atone for his past.

The universal themes of hurt, pain, redemption, atonement, sin, weakness, and forgiveness make this book applicable to everyone. Forgiveness is not just offered by the wounded but by all of those affected by the trauma including those who care for the injured party. The feelings of Dr. Johnson's intimate family members are explored in details not observed in her other books. Although the resolution of her first husband's fate in the series is long awaited, it does not eclipse the other inflicted wounds in this story.

Perhaps one of the most painful and taboo subjects is religious scandals and conflicts. Although the media continues to explore the problems in the ministry, many authors stray away from any formal critique of the ministry. The level of deceit, scandal, hypocrisy, inhumanity, lack of compassion, and manipulation by those who proclaim themselves as spiritually mature leaders explored in this book is just as riveting and surprising as in the fictional book, The Thorn Birds by Colleen McCullough. The Thorn Birds deals with the fall and redemption of a priest from immorality.

The depravity of man is such that at times the reader must accept that reality is more sensational than fiction. Dr. Johnson provides a balanced perspective on the ministry, is able to stray away from bashing those in the pulpit, and offers an honest critique of the church. Dr. Johnson is able to recognize and highlight the positive aspects of the ministry and offer solutions to correct problems in some modern ministries. Her balanced perspective offers hope and promise to heal those wounded by the church. Rather than speaking against God's leaders, she allows the Word to judge, as the prophets of old spoke against corruption in the ministry and brought correction to help the great men of God who were as human and fallible as our current leaders. Dr. Johnson talks from a place of love to help and not to harm so that the love of the Bible is spread and is not overshadowed by the desire to build larger ministries at the expense of the people. Oil for the Wounded discusses Dr. Johnson's personal wounds but also the wounds of others who wanted to share their healing process to edify others. This book is excellent for those who are wounded, need compassion, those who feel dispassionate about life, need redemption, forgiveness, and compassion, and for those who want to help others professionally, informally to recover from wounds, or to redeem themselves from inflicting wounds.

Hurt or Wounded

And went to him, and bound up his wounds,
pouring in oil and wine, and set him on
his own beast, and brought him to an inn,
and took care of him.
Luke 10:34

My great uncle and aunt, Ruben and Hattie Owens, were married over sixty years. In their later years, they both developed health problems. My uncle's problems were more severe than my aunt's health problems. On multiple occasions, the doctors gave up on him. It seemed that he was determined to live. They were residing in a nursing home when Aunt Hattie died.

The night before she passed, I received a call to come to the hospital. They thought that she would pass within the hour. It was difficult for me to decide if my uncle should be told. It was well into the next day and my aunt was still holding on to life. Finally, I decided to bring my uncle to the hospital. For a long period of time, he just sat quietly across the room. Knowing that his health was also frail, I couldn't bring myself to tell him that she was dying. As she lingered somewhere between two worlds, I asked my uncle to come say something to her.

He walked over to the bed, touched her

on her forehead and gently said, "Scrap (his pet name for her), I love you and Charlotte does, too."

My aunt's eyes immediately opened and she was gone. My uncle was able to assist me with making all the arrangements for the funeral. The day after the funeral, I went to see him. When I arrived, he was sitting in a chair next to the heater. He was still wearing the suit that he had worn on the previous day. He was taking the heater apart. Prior to this day, he had shown no signs of dementia.

He heals the brokenhearted
and binds up their wounds.
Psalm 147:3 ESV

Approximately a month later, I received notice that my uncle was at the hospital. When we arrived, he was already gone. The staff at the nursing home said that all day long, he had a conversation with someone they were unable to see. One of the attendants said, as she passed his room, she heard him say, "I'm ready." When she returned a few minutes later, he was gone.

My uncle didn't die from any of the conditions that had plagued him for years. His heart simply stopped. It's my belief that he died from a broken heart; he died from his wounds.

There will be times in each of our lives when we face physical, emotional, psychological, and spiritual hurt. It has been said that into each life some rain will fall. That rain is often equated with pain. Not only will we feel pain, we will cause pain. We will cause hurt to someone else. It is the severity and longevity of pain that will aid in distinguishing between a hurt and a wound.

Church hurt or church wounds are often very severe. It is sometimes the severest form of "friendly fire." It carries guilt, shame, and blame that are often misplaced. Those who have experienced this type of pain often become angry at God and walk away from the church.

The Merriam Webster Dictionary defines hurt as to inflict with physical pain: to do substantial or material harm: to cause emotional pain or anguish to: to be detrimental to: to suffer pain or grief: to be in need: to cause damage or distress

My purpose in writing this book is not to change or challenge that definition. My intention is to explore the topic to expand our growth. The word hurt can be used in a variety of ways and serve various functions within a sentence.

The Merriam Webster Dictionary defines a wound as an injury to the body (as from violence, accident, or surgery) that typically involves laceration or breaking of a membrane (as the skin) and usually damage to underlying tissues: a cut or breach in a plant usually due to an external agent: a mental or emotional hurt or blow: something resembling a wound in appearance or effect; *especially*: a rift in or blow to a political body or social group

By definition, a wound is seen as more severe than a hurt. When thinking of the military, it is often the wounds of the soldiers that come to mind. The very nature of the equipment used by the military leads us to think of the injury as a wound.

Wounds may be caused by friendly or enemy fire. Indeed, sometimes wounds occur accidently. Wounds that occur because of friendly fire are precipitated by someone who is considered a friend or companion in arms. It is extremely difficult to accept these types of wounds. They are unexpected. They can cause doubt, undue speculation, and animosity between friends or comrades.

Hurts are usually temporary. Hurts that go untreated can become wounds. If a hurt goes untreated for an extended period of time, it develops a deep root. The deeper the root, the harder it is to heal the wound. It takes a wise and skillful counselor to facilitate the healing of the wound. It takes a wise person to pour oil into the wound.

Guard your heart above all else, for it
determines the course of your life.
Proverbs 4:23

Wounds are usually accompanied by outward manifestations. Anger, resentment, jealousy, insecurity, paranoia, and a wide range of emotions are often triggered by wounds. Substance abuse, violence, promiscuity, and criminal activities are often the offspring of wounds.

The source of the wound can be difficult to identify. Inexperienced or ill prepared counselors or confidants have the potential to aggravate or worsen the wound. In truth, the healing of the counselor or confidant must come first. Hurt people will hurt people. Wounded people will wound people. Good intentions are not enough to aid healing.

When the death of a spouse occurs, there is grief, hurt, and pain. The grief will manifest in numerous ways. Even unfaithful spouses who have failed to provide the financial and spiritual leadership for their families are mourned. When a faithful, loving, and supportive spouse dies, the pain is often deeper. The grief process may last longer and be more intense. It may create a wound. When couples have been married for an extended period of time, the wounds may be terminal.

In many ways, a divorce is like a death. Losing a beloved job after numerous years can be a form of death. Retirement can be a form of death. These things have the potential to become wounds.

A child's death can be devastating. Even if a child causes grief and pain to the parents, their death can be extremely painful. When a child is a child full of hope and promise, the death can cause a painful wound.

The infidelity of a trusted spouse can be difficult to overcome. Shame and embarrassment will compound the hurt. The greater the trust, the greater the hurt will be. The longer the trust has lasted, the deeper the wound will be.

Is there help for people who suffer from these types of wounds? How can we help? We can start by lovingly caring. Make yourself available for the duration of the flight. It may be a short flight or a long one. Each trip is different. There are no magic tricks to speed up the process. Buckle your seat belts and pray; the ride may get bumpy. Time may be the oil that's needed for the wound.

As pastors, evangelist, teachers, apostles, bishops, friends, family members, neighbors, and Christians, opportunities to provide counseling, support, or advice are inevitable. It is not a role that we can choose to ignore. It is an intricate part of the God-given profession. Even if you are not a professional, opportunities will arise. Some people are so wounded that they will not seek professional or spiritual help.

"I can do nothing on my own. As I hear, I judge, and my judgment is just because I seek not My own will but the will of Him who sent Me.
John 5:30 ESV

Conflicts will inevitably occur within the church, just as they occur elsewhere. When two or more people are gathered together, there is potential for conflict. If these are handled inappropriately, one or more parties will be hurt. The Wisdom of Solomon is needed to solve these conflicts. Pray for this type of wisdom.

Let me be weighed in an even balance, that God may know mine integrity.
Job 31:6

In mediating any conflict, it is wise to use a balanced weight. In the courting phase of any relationship, liberty is often given to the person being courted. A person with more financial resources or assets may be given liberty. A loyal and faithful person may be taken for granted. The feelings of a person who seems more spiritually mature may be discarded. When these unfair balances occur in the body of Christ, wounds occur.

Guard me as you would guard Your own eyes. Hide me in the shadow of Your wings.
Psalm 17:8 NLT

Just as our eyes are precious to us, so are we precious to God. As we protect the pupils of our eyes, so God protects us. We must not conclude that we have missed God's protection if we experience trials or troubles. God's protection has a far greater purpose than just helping us to avoid pain. God allows suffering for numerous reasons. If we allow it, our trials will make us better servants for Him. God also protects us by guiding us through painful circumstances. At other times, He helps us to escape them.

Whenever we experience hurt or pain, we can rest assured that God cares. He understands our hurt, pain, and even our wounds. He has the solution. He has provided oil for the wounded.

Salty Wounds

Singing cheerful songs to a person whose heart is heavy is as bad as stealing someone's jacket in cold weather or rubbing salt in a wound.
Proverbs 25:20 NLT

A young woman came to see me. Prior to meeting me, she called for directions to the place appointed for our meeting. During our very brief conversation, her irritation was apparent. When she arrived, my suspicion was confirmed.

After greeting her, I said, "You are really angry!"

Hotly, she responded, "Yes I am!"

Realizing that the referring problem was only symptomatic of the real problem, I asked, "Why are you so angry?"

She replied, "I don't know!"

In an attempt to gain clarity, I continued, "How long have you been angry?"

With sadness in her tone, she replied, "I don't know! It seems like forever."

When I asked if she was referred to me because of issues with anger management, she responded, "NO! I don't know why I wasn't! When all of this happened, I was really angry. I cursed the police out. It was extremely difficult for them to get me to calm down."

After identifying her issue with anger as being the most pressing need, the root of the anger needed to be identified. After numerous questions, we were able to identify the situation that had affected most of her life. Watching domestic violence during her childhood had changed her disposition. She admitted that she seldom found any reason to smile or laugh. Several other things had added salt to her wound. Feelings of guilt were currently aggravating the wound.

Minor cuts and scrapes usually don't require medical attention or a trip to the emergency room. Still, proper care is essential to avoid infection, irritation, or other complications.

Ye are the salt of the earth: but if the salt have lost his savour, wherewith shall it be salted? it is thenceforth good for nothing but to be cast out, and to be trodden under foot of men.

Matthew 5:13

Salt has varied uses. As the salt of the earth, we are to aid in making the world a better place by helping to heal others. Salt is used to give added flavor to food. Salt is also used in pottery production to

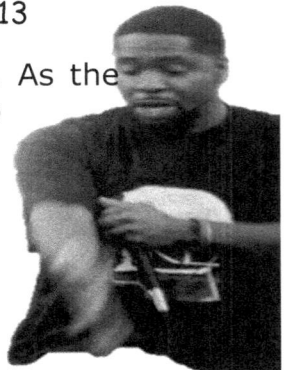

form the very smooth glaze on clay tiles or pottery ware. Salt water can aid the healing of minor scrapes and cuts. It helps to dry the cut. The salt that is applied to meat in order to preserve it is applied in vast amounts.

The famous expression "rubbing salt in the wound" has a negative connotation. To rub salt into the wound is synonymous with adding insult to injury or kicking someone while they are down. The term is derived from the stingingly painful sensation of table salt deliberately being rubbed into an open, bleeding wound. This technique may be used as a form of torture or during hostile interrogations.

Salt tends to sting when placed in an open sore, cut, or wound. Salt water can be beneficial in the long run when properly diluted. Because salt tends to be abrasive, when it is not properly diluted it will cause further irritation. To rub salt into someone's wounds is equivalent to making someone feel even worse about something. You rub their pain or misfortune in. It is essentially doing or saying something to make the situation worse or exaggerated. This type of salt aggravates the wound. Rather than causing healing, it preserves the pain.

When salt has caused irritation to a wound it becomes more difficult to heal. The layer or layers of salt may hide or mask the true problem. It will take time and patience to identify and heal the wound.

As Christians, we use the Word of God to help heal wounds. When the Word is used in a destructive manner to beat someone into submission, we add salt to the wound. When salt irritates the wound, there are other irritants that began to manifest. It can seem easier to focus on the outward symptoms. If the root isn't treated, the problem is likely to reoccur. As Christian's our aim should be to pour oil into the wound, not salt.

Artist: August Burns Red lyrics
Title: White Washed
I won't hesitate to put you in your place.
You are the straw that's crushing my back.
You ask me to be blameless.
You ask me to be blameless but who are you to decide what's right?
Don't say another word...
However, I thank you for this pen and ink ammunition.
Thank you for the inspiration.
You're the straw that's crushing my back.
You are the salt that's burning my wounds.

Wounds Reopened

From the sole of your foot to the top of your head there is no soundness--only wounds and welts and open sores, not cleansed or bandaged or soothed with oil.

Isaiah 1:6 NIV

There is a deep wound in my life. It has been there for most of my life and it was a very destructive force in my life. Although I think the wound has healed, there are times that it appears to reopen for no apparent reason. I refer to it as my daddy issues.

On Wednesday, July 18, 1962, a young soldier took the life of my father. As Herman Russell Jr. sat in his car waiting for a train to clear the railroad tracks, he was brutally murdered. On that summer night in Hopkinsville, Kentucky, my father sat in his car with the windows rolled down. Another soldier approached the car and proceeded to take his life. He stabbed my twenty-five-year-old father numerous times. The perpetrator of the crime was another twenty-two-year-old soldier, Willie High, Jr. It was reported that the young soldiers were involved in an earlier altercation. The circumstances surrounding the incident remain cloudy to me. At the time of this incident, I was three years old.

Periodically, thoughts of my father will overwhelm me. Whereas in times past, I was unable to shake the grief, it doesn't linger now. After a few tears, I acknowledge the pain; a short time later, it leaves for a season. Inevitably, it returns. Today, I don't act out on my grief. Well, that may not be totally honest.

About six years ago, I was sitting in my office with Mama. For no apparent reason, I thought about the man who killed my father. Over the years, I often wondered if he knew what he had done to my life and if he had any understanding of the depth of the pain that he had forced into my life. It was difficult to understand how Mama could forgive the man who had single-handedly wrecked my life. Shortly after murdering my father, the murderer wrote her a letter of apology. Mama quickly accepted his plea for forgiveness. Her forgiveness was a thorn in my flesh for many years.

Suddenly, I wanted to know what happened to this man. After asking Mama a few questions, I located the man. Within five minutes, I was on the telephone with him. After identifying myself, I really didn't have anything to say. He took the lead. Although I was surprised by his words and attitude towards the murder that almost destroyed my life, I remained calm. His actions had caused so much damage and he had no apparent remorse.

With an edge of agitation, he said, "That mess cost me three years of my life!"

If it had only cost me three years of my life, it would have been a welcomed relief. Instead, it extracted a much higher price. As the man continued his attempts to justify the murder, I remained silent. Mama asked for the telephone. I don't know what it is about my mother that makes her so special. There I go again. That's a cliché; I know what makes her so special. It's the God in her. He was there before she gave her life to Him. After identifying herself, she began chatting as if they were old friends. This time, I didn't get angry.

What was my purpose in calling this man? God only knows! Did it provide healing or closure? It provided neither. Has oil been poured into my wound? It has! From time to time, oil has to be poured in again.

July 18, 2012, will mark the fiftieth anniversary of my father's death. Throughout these years, my father has remained the love of my mother's life. It is extremely rare that a week goes by without her mentioning her love for him. It has often bothered me that she was able to forgive the person who took so much from her.

When I asked her to explain how she

was able to do this, she responded, "I have known many emotions; I have never known hate. I have been hurt. I have been disappointed. I have cried but I have never known hate. I wanted him punished for his crime; I never wanted revenge. I wasn't saved but I didn't want bitterness to destroy my life."

From the sole of the foot even to the head, there is no soundness in it but bruises and sores and raw wounds; they are not pressed out or bound up or softened with oil.
Isaiah 1:6 ESV

Over the years, I have worked with a number of programs. God has blessed me to impart into the lives of many of the people who came through these programs. They are my children. They are near and dear to my heart. God gave them to me. Recently, one of my children had a wound reopened.

In 1998, Johnnie A. Worsley was convicted of rape and double murder of a mother and her daughter on March 7, 1995. He received a sentence of life without parole for the rape. For the murders, he received the death sentence. During this time, a surviving daughter was my client.

It was a very difficult time. There were no words to comfort her. Everyone in the program tried to offer support. All we could do was listen to her. She was twenty-one when this happened.

Lashonia described it this way:

He stabbed my sister twenty something times! She never got to finish high school. She never got to have children. She never got to be an aunt to my children. With what he did it changed everything for my life.

A week before he beat my mother with a bat, he threatened to kill my mother. I questioned him about what he said. He said he was just joking. He wasn't! I knew he wasn't joking. My mama just wanted to make her marriage work. She was doing everything she could to make it work.

My children never got to know their aunt. They never got to know their grandmother. He took everything! One of my daughters looks just like my sister.

It took a week for the police to release the house from being a crime scene. We had to go in there. We removed the bloody mattress. It's a scene that I can never forget.

I learned to live with it. Mother's Day has never been the same. My mother was the life of the party.

Thirteen years later, a Superior Court judge ruled in favor of the Columbus man condemned to death for slaying his wife and stepdaughter. The judge ruled that Worsley deserves a new penalty phase trial because his attorneys failed to offer sufficient mitigating evidence to the jury. Worsley pleaded guilty but mentally ill to the double murder and never denied his guilt.

The case that seemed forgotten for years didn't resurface, until recently. Judge Allen ruled Worsley's defense attorneys fell "woefully short" of the effective assistance of counsel standard, essentially depriving him of his constitutional rights. The hearing lasted two days.

Lashonia describes her feelings as the wound was reopened:

> There were so many things and details that I had forgotten. During his trial, I was still in shock. In those two days, I had to relive everything. I had a panic attack. I looked at his hands and I said 'these are the hands that killed my mama. These are the hands that killed my sister.'
>
> I know the judge made his decision on what was before him but we are entitled to something. We are entitled to peace and closure. It's just hard! Now after all these years, he is sitting in jail with basically no sentence. Every time I have to go to that courtroom, I'm back in 1995. It's torture! It's just torture!
>
> That day, I hadn't heard from my mama and my sister all day. I knew they were somewhere together, dead! I just knew it! I told my aunts, 'I know they are dead.'

What do you say when a tragedy like this happens? What can you do or say that will ease the pain? Is there a way to heal this wound so that it will never return? How do you pour oil into this wound?

> He healeth the broken in heart,
> and bindeth up their wounds.
> Psalm 147:3

My children are very diverse. Some of them are older and more mature than I am. In these relationships, age is not a factor. The nature of our relationships elevates them to the status of my children.

Several years ago, I was conducting a workshop for over one hundred people. As I was preparing to start a discussion, several of my children interrupted me. They wanted me to know that one of my children was in the hall crying. It was the anniversary of one of her daughters' death. The topic of discussion was suddenly changed.

After escorting my grieving child back into the room, I seated her at a table near the front of the room. Across from her, I placed another chair. Afterward I asked her to provide me with the most recent pictures of her daughters before their passing.

As she was providing the pictures, she continuously cried, "I never had the chance to say goodbye!"

With the pictures in my hands, I walked through the audience looking for someone with a resemblance to each daughter. Two women in the audience bore a strong resemblance to the pictures. When asked if they would assist me, they quickly agreed.

The first woman was asked to take the seat across from the grieving mother. She was also asked to hold the picture up. The grieving mother was provided an opportunity to say everything that she wished to say to her daughter. As she finished talking to her first daughter, the second young woman took the seat. The same pattern was repeated. As the mother completed her goodbyes, each young woman responded.

With tears streaming down their face, they each said, "I love you, Mama! Now, release me!"

As the conversation was progressing, the room was growing more emotional. One young woman ran down the aisle screaming, "My baby died! I have been mad at God since it happened!" This opened up a flood gate and others began to share their wounds. By the time the session ended, oil had been poured into multiple wounds. Many were on their way to healing. It isn't always this simple or this easy. Everyone is not ready to heal; these were ready. Prayerfully, you can take this step today. Allow God to pour oil into your wound.

Lost in Black and White

A simple man believes anything but a prudent
man gives thought to his steps.
Proverbs 14:15 NIV

There are many who can only see the
world in black or white. They miss the
beautiful shades of gray and the shadows of
cream and tan. They only see life as right or
wrong. They see good or evil. They see win
or lose. They see the truth or a lie. They see
near or far. They see now or later. They are
unable to see that there are no simple
answers.

The Bible tells us to let your yea be yea
and your nay, nay. It tells us that a double-
minded man is unstable in all his ways. It
further states, "Oh how I wish you were hot
or cold." In matters of righteousness, our
stand should be firm and sure.

Let the word of Christ richly dwell within you,
with all wisdom teaching and admonishing one
another with psalms and hymns and spiritual
songs, singing with thankfulness
in your hearts to God.
Colossians 3:16 NAS

There are other times when the
answers aren't clear. The Bible may not

make a specific reference to a situation. There are times when we will face situations where we will need to judge with righteous judgment. What happens when our deductive reasoning skills are limited? What happens if our ability to discern truth is impaired?

A rainbow has many beautiful colors. We can appreciate its beauty. With a rainbow, two people may see the colors differently. It is often difficult to determine where one color ends and another begins. This can be said of truth. Two people may experience the same situation but see totally different shades of truth. Each person will interpret truth based on their intellectual ability, spiritual insight, and past experiences.

"How long, you simpletons, will you insist on being simpleminded? How long will you mockers relish your mocking? How long will you fools hate knowledge?
Proverbs 1:22 NIV

Things aren't always what they appear to be. When there are disagreements, rather than being a lie, it may be a difference in perception. It may be a misunderstanding of the facts. In order to arrive at the truth, you will have to discern the facts. You will have to hear the meta-messages. These are the non-verbal messages. These are often the greatest indicators of the truth.

It can be extremely difficult to have a rational conversation with a person who sees life only in black and white. They may lack the ability to rationalize. As you attempt to help them understand, you will become frustrated. For them, life is very simple. They may become confused. How can you get them to understand what you are saying? Except God reveals truth to them, they may never come to the knowledge of the truth.

My mother has wise sayings that she shares. This is one of them, "You may be arguing with a fool but the people who are watching don't know the difference."

I read in the newspaper of a man who was arrested after he was observed in the middle of the street, fighting with himself. He was reportedly jumping, yelling, and fighting. When he was questioned by officers, he said that he was arguing with his associates. Police report that no one else was nearby.

We often assume that a person is deliberately choosing to be disagreeable. However, the person may sincerely lack the ability to comprehend the situation. They may believe what they see or hear is truth and be unable to analyze the information.

A person who lacks the ability to see in color will be hurt. They will have difficulty comprehending truth because they rely on what they have heard. They often have a good memory. Their memories interfere with their ability to learn and discover truth. They may even resist learning new information because they are afraid to trust their ability to discern the truth. Because they lack the ability to apply critical thinking, they will not see the potential consequences of their actions. They will cause hurt to others without realizing it.

Wisdom is the principal thing; therefore get
wisdom: and with all thy getting
get understanding.
Proverbs 4:7

Wisdom begins with accepting the salvation offered through Christ. A Christian without wisdom and grace is a dangerous one. Wisdom is a necessity. Understanding in this verse comes from Christ. If any man lacks wisdom, let them ask of God.

When seeking counsel or direction from a person who lacks spiritual insight or discernment, problems are often made worse. Rather than resolving conflicts, conflicts are exaggerated. Rather than healing hurts, wounds are created. Rather than pouring oil on a wound, salt finds its way into the wound.

The Sacred Pulpit

And the LORD said unto him, I have heard thy prayer and thy supplication, that thou hast made before Me: I have hallowed this house, which thou hast built, to put My name there for ever; and Mine eyes and Mine heart shall be there perpetually.

1 Kings 9:3

I certainly don't put forth myself as a paragon of perfect virtue. More than once, I have stumbled on this Christian path. My heart has never stumbled away from God. Certainly during my Christian walk, I have said more than one thing that I would like to retrieve. In relation to language in the pulpit, I've made my mistakes, said things poorly, and have said things I regret. In spite of this, I can say I have always tried to remember that I was speaking for a Holy God, from the precious Word of God. It is a blessed privilege and honor to stand behind what I have always been told is "sacred."

"The people of Judah have sinned before my very eyes," says the LORD. "They have set up their abominable idols right in the Temple that bears My name, defiling it.
Jeremiah 7:30 NLT

A pulpit is a sacred place and thus should be treated with the highest degree of propriety and respect. I am in favor of making every effort to enhance communication. Tools of good communication can enhance the power of the preached Word under the anointing of the Holy Spirit. It appears that some have forgotten the sacredness of the pulpit and the altar.

Then I will go to the altar of God, To God my exceeding joy ; And upon the lyre I shall praise You, O God, my God.
Psalm 43:4 NAS

Crudity in the pulpit really disturbs me. Profanity, toilet humor, and sexually explicit language now seem to be2 acceptable to some pastors. They call it being real. I call it being raw. Our Lord and Savior deserves to be represented with dignity by the person and their vocabulary. The messenger does not have to lower the dignity of the pulpit in order to communicate the gospel or even to give a stinging rebuke of sin.

Love wisdom like a sister; make insight a beloved member of your family. Let them protect you from an affair with an immoral woman, from listening to the flattery of a promiscuous woman.
Proverbs 7:4-5 NLT

Sexual education should be taught in our homes and our churches. It is not something that should be left to the schools. Parents should take the lead in sex education. This education should occur in a responsible manner and consistent with Biblical guidelines. It should not be crude or vulgar.

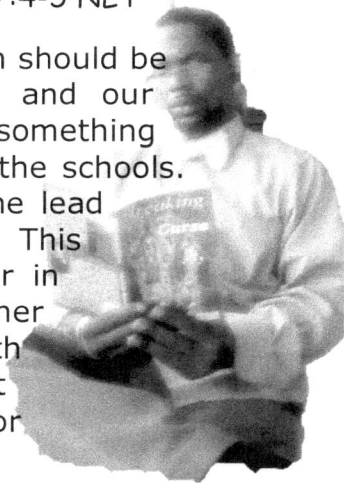

Moreover all the chief of the priests, and the people, transgressed very much after all the abominations of the heathen; and polluted the house of the LORD which He had hallowed in Jerusalem.
2 Chronicles 36:14

When the tongue is not controlled by the Holy Spirit, the sacredness of the pulpit is often desolated. The tongue is not controlled by the Holy Spirit because the heart is not right or preparation has not been made. It is always proper to speak and exhort the text. When a speaker digresses from the Biblical text, the principles of the Word of God may be violated. Speech should always be gracious, seasoned with salt.

> They must be silenced because they are ruining whole households by teaching things they ought not to teach--and that for the sake of dishonest gain.
> Titus 1:11

Crude and vulgar comments about sex have no godly place in the pulpit. We should truly ask the Holy Spirit to lead us in our preaching and be sure that it involves no coarse jesting that might make people laugh but grieve the Holy Spirit.

2nd Peter chapter 2 speaks plainly of false prophets. Peter tells us how to detect them. He gives us two things to look for: greed and sensual lust. He covers greed in verses 3 and 14 and spends the rest of the chapter discussing the false teachers' lust problems. This type of language stirs up the problem of lust!

Let the godly strike me! It will be a kindness! If they correct me, it is soothing medicine. Don't let me refuse it. But I pray constantly against the wicked and their deeds.

Psalm 141:5 NLT

The pulpit has been used on too many occasions to abuse God's people. As a survivor of extreme domestic violence, I have a problem accepting abuse in any form. Verbal abuse compounded by spiritual abuse causes serious wounds. On more than one occasion, I left a church that I sincerely loved because of this type of abuse. While not directed directly towards me, the pain was intense.

The house of God is designed as a place of healing. It was never meant to be a war zone. Rather than watch as the people of God were assaulted and wounded by friendly fire, I chose to make a hasty exit. When friendly fire is aimed at the pastor, I do the same. Stray bullets have wounded many people. When physical, verbal, or spiritual fighting ensues, I make an exit.

There are those who would insist that this type of correction is necessary to maintain order in the church. Order in any organization is a necessity. The Bible has orderly ways to handle disputes. It never says beat them from the pulpit. Love and kindness are always in order.

The mild and humble manner in which Paul addresses the Corinthians is an example for us. It is his desire that he will not need to use harsh words with them. In the midst of his greatest provocations, Paul shows humility and meekness. Paul follows the example from Christ of meekness and gentleness.

Now I, Paul, plead with you. I plead with the gentleness and kindness that Christ Himself would use, even though some of you say I am bold in my letters but timid in person. I hope it won't be necessary but when I come I may have to be very bold with those who think we act from purely human motives.
2 Corinthians 10:1-2 NLT

When we find ourselves tempted to be harsh towards anybody, we should remember the meekness and gentleness of Christ. Bitter and sweet water were never meant to flow from the same fountain. The sweet water provides healing for the wounds of the people. It is bitter water flowing from the same source that has often caused the wound. It is time for reverence to return to the sacred pulpit. The oil that flows from this holy ground has been tainted long enough.

For Your Glory

Tell everyone about God's power. His majesty
shines down on Israel; His strength is mighty in
the heavens. God is awesome in His sanctuary.
The God of Israel gives power and strength to
His people. Praise be to God!
Psalm 68:34-35, NLT

Nature surrounds us with countless
signs of God's wonderful power. His
unlimited power and His unspeakable
majesty leave us breathless and awe inspired
in His presence.
How blessed we are
that God cares for
us in spite of our
imperfections. When
we consider all God
has done for us, we
should feel an
overwhelming sense
of awe as we kneel
before the Lord in His holy sanctuary.

The LORD is a friend to those who fear Him. He
teaches them His covenant.
Psalm 25:14 NLT

The LORD confides in those who fear
Him." Our Father God offers intimate and

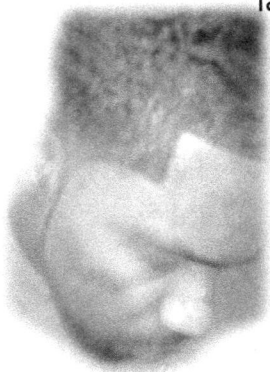

lasting friendship to all who reverence Him, who hold Him in the highest honor, and who esteem Him above all others. What relationship could ever compare with having the Lord of all creation for a friend? Your everlasting friendship with God will grow as you revere Him. He is the friend that loves us unselfishly and unconditionally.

Serve the LORD with reverent fear, and rejoice with trembling. Submit to God's royal son, or He will become angry, and you will be destroyed in the midst of all your activities--for His anger flares up in an instant. But what joy for all who take refuge in Him!
Psalm 2:11-12, NLT

We must surrender fully to the authority of God and His dear son, Jesus. We must fully submit to His Son. Christ is God's only chosen King. God never wanted His people to serve an earthly king. The Jews wanted to be like other nations and demanded a king. God viewed this as rejection of His rule and authority. Jesus is also the rightful King over our hearts and lives.

"You shall not make for yourself an idol, or any likeness of what is in heaven above or on the earth beneath or in the water under the earth. You shall not worship them or serve them; for I, the LORD your God, am a jealous God"
Exodus 20:4-5

God is a jealous God. When the term jealousy is applied to God in scripture, it is usually because His people are worshiping idols. In His ten commandments, He warned His people not to worship anything or anyone else but they failed to listen. God is not willing to share His glory with anyone else. The higher we lift and exalt men, the lower we attempt to bring God down from His throne.

"But let him that glories glory in this, that he understands and knows Me, that I am the LORD which exercise loving-kindness, judgment, and righteousness, in the earth: for in these things I delight", says the LORD.
Jeremiah 9:24 NIV

If we are seriously committed to our relationship with Him, we will exalt Him above everyone and everything else in our lives. We will be totally and completely dedicated to living for His honor. We will also be zealously committed to obeying His will for our lives. The primary goal of our lives will be to show the world that our God is the one true and living God.

Ye therefore, beloved, seeing ye know these things before, beware lest ye also, being led away with the error of the wicked, fall from your own steadfastness. But grow is grace, and in the knowledge of our Lord and Saviour Jesus Christ. To Him be glory both now and for ever" 2 Peter 3:17-18

To be ready for Christ's return, we must submit to His leadership. He is to be highly exalted and lifted up. We are to point people to Jesus and not to ourselves. We are to provide Him with all the love, adoration, respect, honor, and reverence He deserves.

If people are to be healed from their wounds, they will need a proper revelation of who Jesus is. This will be the foundation for their healing. No other person can provide the stability that is needed for restoration to wholeness. When the pulpit and altar are set aside for this purpose, there is healing oil there for the wounded.

Proper Reproof

All Scripture *is* given by inspiration of God, and *is* profitable for doctrine, for reproof, for correction, for instruction in righteousness,
2 Timothy 3:16 NKJV

There is a story that I heard. A pastor was assigned to a new church. The members didn't like the pastor's style of preaching. When one member was asked what he was preaching about, the member replied, "He's condemning everybody to hell!" This pastor was removed and replaced by another one. The people loved the new pastor. The same member was asked what the new pastor was preaching about, he replied, "His message condemning everybody to hell!" This left the person confused. He asked, "Well, what is the difference?" The member replied, "When the first pastor was condemning everybody to hell, he seemed to enjoy it. When the new pastor is condemning everybody to hell, he does it with tears streaming down his face."

The method does make all the difference. The right to challenge behavior has to be earned. When people know that you love them, they are more likely to take correction. My mother often says, "People don't care how much you know, until they know how much you care."

Paul penned 2 Timothy to leave his beloved son in the faith with words to establish firmly the function of the Word of God in his life and for future believers. Paul's often quoted passage regarding the profitable use of scripture is directed at Timothy, not at others, (*"But YOU..."* 3:14). Paul's desire is not that Timothy would use the scripture to bring offense to others. Paul never envisioned this as an excuse to berate and overwhelm God's people. Verbal abuse is wrong in any arena. It leaves not only invisible scars but also visible wounds.

The effects of verbal abuse are often obvious. A lack of self-esteem, a lack of self-confidence, suicidal ideations, violence, and substance abuse are often direct byproducts of verbal abuse. The damage is often difficult to heal. Those who have suffered from this villain often crave love, affection, and attention. Until the damage is repaired, their insecurities are never satisfied.

Paul tells Timothy to, *"Convince, rebuke, and exhort"* others but reinforces this charge by adding the words, *"with all long-suffering and teaching."* This is a different standard than when applying scripture to self. Be brutal when applying God's Word to your own life but exercise grace, mercy, love, self-control, and sound teaching when applying it to others.

And do you think this, O man, you who judge
those practicing such things, and doing the
same, that you will escape the judgment of God?
Or do you despise the riches of His goodness,
forbearance, and longsuffering,
not knowing that the goodness of God
leads you to repentance?
Romans 2:3-4 NKJV

As Paul instructed, we are to teach the Word and allow God to do the rest. God said His word will not return void but it will accomplish what He pleases. If we preach the Word, the Word will do the reproof. Preaching is never to be done in a harsh uncaring way but in love. God gives the increase in all things. The desire for lasting change will come from His spirit bringing conviction.

Galatians 6:1 tells us if a brother be overtaken in sin, you who are spiritual restore him with gentleness, lest you be tempted also. God brings conviction. Man brings condemnation. Paul stresses "ye who are spiritual" because people who are not spiritual often bring condemnation and lack the ability to bring restoration.

When people encounter Christians, they should leave the interaction feeling stronger. They should leave empowered for service. If people leave feeling dejected or despondent after conversing with us, something is wrong. This is not to say everyone will accept help. However, I am saying that hurting people shouldn't feel worse after conferring with Christians.

Let your speech always be with grace, as though seasoned with salt, so that you will know how you should respond to each person.
Colossians 4:6 NAS

The Bible is also intended for correction. There are those who say that only certain people are to be corrected. Many would even advocate that false teachers are off limits. Christians must use the Word of God to confront false teaching. Many people who don't have a proper interpretation of the Bible may have good intentions. Whatever their intentions are, people who wrongly interpret the Word need to be Biblically corrected. They are teaching others to misinterpret the scriptures. Many souls are in danger.

Priscilla and Aquila heard Apollos sincerely preaching. His doctrine was seriously flawed. He was preaching the truth according to his limited understanding. They pulled him aside and showed him a more excellent way. Christians must show through the Bible a more excellent way for those who are in error. When we allow the Holy Spirit to use us to teach the Bible, we can correct many who are in error. This is always done in a spirit of meekness and love. We don't wink at false teachings. God takes His Word seriously and we should take it seriously, too.

The Word is profitable for instruction in righteousness. We are all on this journey together. We are sinners saved by grace. We all need to be students of God's word. The only book that can give us divine and impartial instructions in godly and righteous living is the Bible. There are many good books but the Bible is our primary source for instructions in righteousness. The Bible provides us with the path God wants us to take.

As we have said before, so I say again now if any man is preaching to you a gospel contrary to what you received, he is to be accursed!
Galatians 1:9 NAS

There are some who say that we are not to discuss the flaws of those who claim to be Christian leaders. There is a measure of truth to this view. We discuss the strengths

56

and weaknesses of political and social leaders. We discuss the weaknesses of our bosses, spouses, children, and our parents. We discuss Abraham, Cain, Absalom, Peter, and Paul. What is the difference? We choose not to discuss the weaknesses of our idols.

David was Israel's second and greatest king. God said that he was *the apple of His eye*. Yet, who has not heard the story of David and Beersheba. Did not God send Nathan to rebuke the king? Nathan loved David. He loved him enough to tell him the truth. This truth brought David back into right standing with God.

Am I saying pastors, elders, leaders, bosses, or anyone in a position of authority should be rebuked lightly or irrelevantly? Absolutely NOT! We should never rebuke anyone without a spirit of love prevailing. Our motives and heart's intents should always be pure. Nothing should be done for vain glory or self-serving purposes. When the right thing is done for the wrong reason, it is still wrong. Let us take careful examination to make sure that our hearts are pure.

But among you it will be different. Those who are the greatest among you should take the lowest rank, and the leader should be like a servant.
Luke 22:26 NLT

This verse states a view that is unlike

what many religions practice today. According to many Christians, a leader has special privileges and is exalted above the members of their congregation and anyone else. Many leaders accept and encourage the exaltation. This is extremely **dangerous**! When we lift anyone up in God's place, we set them up for failure. It also places us in a place to be deeply wounded.

"But be not ye called Rabbi: for one is your Master, even Christ; and all you are brethren. And call no man your father upon the earth, for one is your Father, who is in heaven"
Matthew 23:8-9

God is still a jealous God. He wants our fondest desires and thoughts to be of Him. The greater we exalt anyone the deeper the wound will be that severs this ungodly attachment.

For a number of years, my mother taught Bible study and Sunday school. One night, she was teaching Bible study. She shared a revelation of the Word that God had given her. Although the revelation was

supported by scripture, a young man in his early twenties took offense. Mama was old enough to be his grandmother.

As everyone watched in shock and disbelief, he said, "I don't believe God would have told you that! He would have shown it to the pastor first!"

It was difficult but I contained my response. The pastor wasn't present but his wife was. Normally, she was a very quiet woman. She rose quickly to her feet. Her mouth was still hanging open. She realized that this young man's outburst was an outflow of the pastor's teachings.

She stated very boldly, "The pastor is the pastor of the church but he is not God. There is nothing that prevents God from speaking to other people..."

The LORD lives, and blessed be my rock; And exalted be the God of my salvation,
Psalm 18:46 NAS

After she finished her comments, one of the Elders read the scripture reference that supported Mama's comments. Convinced that God would speak directly to his pastor before he spoke to anyone else, this young man exalted his pastor to a place of extreme authority. He was convinced that revelation knowledge only came through this pastor. He was very vocal in expressing his belief.

One day, the young man learned that the pastor had done something sinful that affected the young man's personal life. He was deeply wounded. Because his exaltation was extreme, the hurt was extreme. He became angry with the pastor, the church, and God. In recent years, I have heard no reports that he has renewed his relationship with God. He needs oil for his wounds. His wounds are deep and have been sustained for years.

Christ teaches us that our leadership should be different than what the world portrays. We should never boast about being above anyone else. Our positions in life are to be used help others. The greatest leaders or teachers are the ones who can admit that they are in error. They acknowledge that they don't know all the answers. Because they are good leaders, they will work to the correct answers. They endeavor to lead people down the right path.

Examine the leadership examples in our society. Are they examples of humbleness or haughtiness? Examine your own leadership style. If you are a parent, how do you lead your children? If you are a wife, are you insulted by the idea of serving your husband? Sarah called Abraham lord. Husbands, are you able to respect your wives? Are you willing to cover her in prayer?

Service is more than just a sign of humility. It is a sign of love as well. Godly leadership requires love and servitude. This love originates with the love of God. It is the kind love that only God provides. Only God can enable us to love unselfishly.

God is willing to give us the love that will empower us to serve His people. If you struggle in this area, ask God for His love to empower and guide your leadership ability. Ask Him for the kind of love that will strengthen your relationships with people. Follow His example. He is our ultimate servant-leader. As Martin Luther King, Jr. said, "Everybody can be great because everybody can serve!"

One Sunday, after being particularly hard on my husband, God revealed to me the transgression of my ways. He had promised me that if I went to bed, without continuously worrying him, he would go to church with me the next day. He wanted to be left alone to finish getting high, without me 'blowing' (ruining) the high. I left him alone. The next morning, he didn't follow through on his promise. Angrily, I began quoting scriptures to him. He gave no indication he heard one word; therefore, I gave him additional scriptures. He never gave any response.

We were taking communion that

Sunday at church. Prior to taking of the Lord's Supper, the pastor instructed us to search ourselves to see if we were worthy to partake of the supper. As I sat there asking God to search my heart, a voice whispered to me.

"You're not worthy. In love and kindness have I drawn thee. What you just did caused a deep hurt."

My husband had shown no signs he ever heard a word that I said to him. God gently reminded me, it is with kindness and love that He draws men to Him. My intentions were good; my words were taken directly from the Word of God. The scriptures hadn't been taken out of context. Nonetheless, I had carefully chosen each scripture to force my husband to see his wretchedness. Each time he didn't respond to my words, a firmer scripture pronouncing judgment was quoted. My words had been sharp and they had pierced him to the bone.

God's word is never to be used to inflict harm or pain on His children. His word is never to be used for selfish motives or agendas. His Word should never be handled carelessly or irrelevantly. When we say that we represent God, our words represent Him. The words spoken from our lips have the ability to speak hope, faith, life, inspiration, praise, and encouragement.

The lips that speak these words can be used for evil. They can speak gloom, despair, misery, cursing, discouragement, and death. Mama often says, "Please make my words sweet for tomorrow I may have to eat them." After harsh words have been released, they cannot be recaptured. After the damage has been done extensive efforts are often made to correct or justify the damage. This is a difficult task. It is easier to just to remain quiet when we are angry or vexed. It is almost guaranteed that too much will be said. When threats and insults are released, they aggravate the situation.

Words often cause deep wounds that are invisible to the natural eye. They may go untreated. There will always be problems in the church, the workplace, families, society, the home, and the world. This is nothing new. We don't negate our responsibilities because there are wounds. Unforgiveness hinders our growth. My choice is to forgive all who have wounded me. My freedom depends on this oil.

Our words should be seasoned with grace. Our words are meant to bring healing and restoration. Our words should provide oil for the wounded. God cares about our pain and He wants to heal our wounds. He wants to pour oil into our wounds. He has servants who have been called to this task.

Godly Correction

"Now it happened afterward that David's heart troubled him because he had cut Saul's robe. And he said to his men, The LORD forbid that I should do this thing to my master, the Lord's anointed, to stretch out my hand against him, seeing he is the anointed of the LORD"
1 Samuel 24:5-6

After King Saul's disobedience to God, he remained as the anointed King over Israel for some time. Saul became jealous of the heir to his throne, David. He began a relentless manhunt to kill him. At one point, David and his men stumbled across Saul encamped in a cave and had the opportunity to kill the sleeping king. As evidence of his unwillingness to slay Saul, David chose to cut off a portion of Saul's robe. David could have easily justified killing Saul.

"There is neither evil nor transgression
in my hand,
1 Samuel 24:11

Later, the Lord convicted David's heart that not only was it wrong to slay God's anointed; it was also wrong to cut his robe. David repents. Later in this same chapter, David bows his face to the ground. This is a show of humility and respect towards Saul. He then proceeds to rebuke Saul for accusing him falsely. He proclaims his innocence. David strives to convince Saul that he doing an evil thing in pursuing him. He never repents for rightly rebuking Saul. What was the difference? His heart's intent!

Thus saith the LORD of hosts, Hearken not unto the words of the prophets that prophesy unto you: they make you vain: they speak a vision of their own heart, and not out of the mouth of the LORD.
Jeremiah 23:16

A woman went to a revival. She received a word of prophecy. At least, that is what it was supposed to be. The next day, she was really excited. She decided to share her good news with my mother.

She exclaimed, "He told me I was going to have more wisdom than Solomon!"

Without hesitation, my mother chimed in, "You are not going to like me! That is not according to the Word of God! The Bible says that no one who lived before Solomon or after him would have the Wisdom of Solomon. Jesus Christ is the only one who had more wisdom than Solomon!"

The lady dropped her head. She had failed to mark the example of the Berean Christians. If it doesn't line up with the Word, it's not from God. In the Old Testament, false prophecy would result in the death of the false prophets. False prophesies are no laughing matter. God takes seriously the things we say in His name.

"Now these were more noble-minded than those in Thessalonica, for they received the word with great eagerness, examining the Scriptures daily, to see whether these things were so. Many of them therefore believed, along with a number of prominent Greek women and men."
Acts 17:11-12

It is the duty and a great honor for every Christian in holding the leadership of the church accountable. It is our duty to examine their teaching against the Word of God. We should follow the effective example of the Bereans. We are to guard the trust and truth of God's word by lovingly holding our Elders accountable. Loyalty should first be to the Lord and His Word. Loyalty to the creature should never be above that to the Creator. If your pastors are *rightly dividing the Word of truth, a workman that needeth not be ashamed, approved unto God,* then you can rejoice in the Lord for them and their ministry in your life.

Because we are fallen people saved by grace, we should stay open to the constructive criticisms of others. This is particularly true for those who are teachers of the Word. It is possible that a pastor might even unwittingly be skewed or repulsive in what he is teaching from the Word. He may need the gentle yet faithful evaluation from the congregation.

It is customary when attending workshops, seminars, lectures, and classes in a professional environment to provide evaluation forms at the end of the sessions. Many companies provide customer satisfaction surveys. Why is this done? Is it to lower the quality of the presentation? It is done for the exact opposite reason. Constructive criticism and feedback help to improve the quality of the product. Feedback will not improve or tarnish the Bible. It can potentially improve the quality of the presentation. Who is afraid of feedback? Those who fail to realize the value of a multitude of godly counselors are afraid of feed-back.

Paul called the Bereans of "more noble character" because they examined "whether the things Paul taught were so." Their noble character suggests that they are godly counselors. Paul in his wisdom was not insulted or offended by their actions. He welcomed their feedback. He wanted to preserve the integrity of his message. The lens of truth is always the Word of God.

Paul not only thanks the Bereans, he admonishes them to continue to verify the validity of what they are taught. He strongly invites and welcomes scrutiny and evaluation from those in the church. What humility; what transparency; what a selfless motive; what a God-driven agenda; what teachability; what focus; what wisdom; what accountability; what an example for us to follow.

Paul became zealous in his quest to root out those whom he believed had come against orthodox religion. He believed these new converts had erred in their faith; he was wrong. These believers had received direct revelation from God. The Word of God is the acid-test of any revelation. If the revelation cannot be supported by the Word, it is not from God. It is not a true prophecy.

One night, I was in a local restaurant

with one of my friends. A woman from another state asked to join us. After joining us, she immediately began to prophesy to me. They were not general prophecies.

Beloved, do not believe every spirit but test the spirits to see whether they are from God, for many false prophets have gone out into the world.
1 John 4:1 ESV

After approximately twenty minutes, she said, "You recognize false prophets. You often expose them but God is calling you to do more. You need to tell them when they prophesy false prophecies."

Within days, something strange happened. One of my friends was experiencing some very deep, hurtful, and emotionally painful problems. In an effort to pour oil into her wounds, I counseled her extensively. I also recommended that she watch some of the *Three Stooges'* movies; she needed to laugh.

Later that night, we attended a church service with a friend. The pastor of the church allowed someone else to minister. As the service was nearing an end, the pastor walked over to me and began to say several things to me. Both of my friends were standing behind me. My eyes bulged from their sockets when the pastor said openly to me that I was experiencing many devastating things. Not only did she call out everything my friend had shared with me, she said some additional things. Granted, my life is colorful; but, this was a relatively calm period. To top it off, she told me that I needed to laugh and watch some Three Stooges' movies.

This situation was very confusing, hurtful, and embarrassing. The level of the problems dictated that any prophet should not speak them openly. When people have severe wounds, openly exposing the wound pours salt into the wound. Our messages need to be delivered wisely. The second problem was that I laugh almost constantly. It is a gift that God gave me. People often identify me by the sound of my laughter. Many say that I laugh too much.

One thing have I desired of the LORD, that will I seek after; that I may dwell in the house of the LORD all the days of my life, to behold the beauty of the LORD, and to enquire in His temple.
Psalm 27:4

It is extremely rare for anyone to prophesy to me; I do not accept vague and general prophecies. Prophecy is not something that I actively seek. After pondering and searching for any trace of truth in the words spoken by the pastor, I was unable to find any. Joe and a friend recommended that I discuss this with the pastor. Almost immediately, the pastor walked into the building. As I respect this pastor, I went to her in a spirit of humility. My concerns were shared with her.

She responded, "Our desire is not to confuse anybody. That's not good! I'll get with the prophet to verify the validity of what was said and I'll get back with you."

In the past, she had shared some true things with me; but this time, there was not a measure of truth in her words. The prophet said very little. The little that he said was accurate. As she was prophesying to me, he sent someone to lay hands on my friend, who was experiencing these problems.

Two weeks passed and I didn't hear anything from the pastor. One day, I ran into her. She made no mention of what had happened. The next day, in a different location, I saw her with the prophet. She waved at me from a distance. She has not poured oil into that wound.

He will yet fill your mouth with laughter, and
your lips with shouting.
Job 8:21 ESV

God has given me the power to pour oil into many of my wounds. It is through laughter. Once, a former supervisor met with me about my laughter.

The very serious minded woman, asked, "Why is it that you laugh so much? Is it a sign of nervousness?"

This question was never directly answered. Truthfully, prior to my salvation, I smoked marijuana almost constantly. It enabled me to laugh. When I recommitted my life to Christ, He gave me something extra, a natural high.

A joyful heart is good medicine,
but a crushed spirit dries up the bones.
Proverbs 17:22 ESV

In an effort to appease my supervisor who seldom laughed, I did not laugh for a week. During that week, I dealt with people who had been raped, molested, abused, homeless, HIV positive, and addicted to drugs.

One night as I was washing my hair, a floodgate opened. Tears began to pour from me. It seemed I would be unable to stop. I feared that I was having a nervous breakdown. It was not my personal problems that weighed me down; it was the problems of my children. After a long and painful period, the tears stopped.

This happened during the time that I was working on my Master's degree. When I went to class the next night, God poured oil into my wounds. The topic of the lecture that night was *The Power of Laughter*. There were many serious minded people who were unable to appreciate the professor and his antics. Since that night, I have never tried to suppress my laughter. When things seem most difficult, I reach for it.

The rich rules over the poor, and the borrower is the slave of the lender.
Proverbs 22:7 ESV

Once, I heard someone say, "You are going to be blessed beyond measure! When you finish college, you are going to walk into the bank and they are going to be so impressed that you got your Master's degree so young; they are going to loan you a million dollars."

People started clapping and dancing. It seemed that I was the only person thinking, "How many people in the last hundred years received their Master's before age twenty-five? How much interest is on a million dollar loan? How much is the note on that? Does the bank really lend out that kind of money without credit or collateral? How many people are struggling to make student loan payments after finishing college? If it's a blessing can somebody just give it to me without the sorrow? Maybe I just don't have enough faith!"

We are not to dwell on every imperfection of our leaders for that would be unkind, unprofitable, and unloving. We are to encourage them in godly living and maintaining a good reputation within and outside of the church. We are to warn them when we see danger approaching.

Many good pastors have also quit the ministry because of abuse. A minster that I know and respect has been abused by his congregation at more than one church. He is highly educated, possessing multiple advanced degrees. His doctrine and teaching are biblically sound. He is a humble man whose messages are seasoned with grace and love. It has been a pleasure and an honor to have an opportunity to listen to his teaching.

At the first church that he pastored, the abuse from some members of the congregation was so severe that his wife never wanted him to pastor again. After years away from pastoring, he was asked to pastor a large church. There were many benefits to this position at a thriving ministry. Because his wife's wounds were deep, it was an extremely difficult decision to make. After continuous prayer, he reluctantly agreed to take the position. His wife supported his decision. She also became active in the church.

Just as Jannes and Jambres opposed Moses, so also these men oppose the truth--men of depraved minds, who, as far as the faith is concerned, are rejected.
2 Timothy 3:8

Sadly, a few years later, a group of Elders in the church stirred up contention in the ministry. Using deceptive tactics with the church members, they gained the support of the membership to release the pastor from his position. After removing the pastor, a board of Elders assumed control of the ministry. As their ungodly actions were motivated by selfish reasons, they began to bicker among themselves. Church members and the membership were wounded in the midst of this infighting. The church and its academy closed.

We are to cover leaders with prayer. We are to encourage them to faithfully teach God's Word. We are to examine what they are teaching. Paul says, *"Test all things and cling to that which is good..."* However, we are not to wound godly leaders. Paul is the greatest pastor the church has known. Yet, he welcomed scrutiny and accountability.

When I was very new in my walk with the Lord, I believed that every person who attended church was a Christian. I expected them to be kind, loving, and full of compassion. It was a painful lesson to learn that this is not always true.

One Sunday as I was leaving church, I was walking out on my crutches behind two older women. At the time, I assumed that they were in their late eighties or early nineties. I was close enough to hear their conversation.

One of the women turned to the other and sarcastically said, "The devil sure preached a good sermon!"

This shocked me. It was at this same church that I attended my first church meeting. The pastor sat calmly as the deacons hurled continuous accusations at him. It left an extreme distaste in my mouth that has never gone away; I hate church meetings. Throughout the meeting, I was thinking, "When I get out of here, I am never coming back." Although I left that church, I have occasionally visited the church. Since that night, there have been numerous pastors assigned to that church. After almost thirty years, it is still almost impossible to get me to attend a church meeting.

O LORD, You have searched me and known me. You know when I sit down and when I rise up; You

understand my thought from afar. You scrutinize my path and my lying down, And are intimately acquainted with all my ways.
Psalm 139:1-3 NAS

How can we remain humble and assist our pastors? How can we bring that critical observation to our pastors in a humble and loving way? How can we bring correction to our pastors in a way that not only serves him but pleases and honors God? This is not to address sins that would disqualify a pastor from ministry. These sins should be addressed by a higher spiritual authority.

We should examine our hearts prior to any conversation in which we bring correction or rebuke. Motive, method, and attitude make the difference. It is wise for us to examine our hearts for any hint of impureness or self-righteousness. This should not only be done with our interactions with the pastor, it is a good practice with anyone. Is my desire to share this critical observation with my pastor motivated by a desire to serve? Is it motivated by love? We must not assume our motive is humble and redemptive. Our purpose must be to serve our pastor, not to scold them. The next step is to pray again.

Do not receive an accusation against an elder

except on the basis of two or three
witnesses. Those who continue in sin, rebuke in
the presence of all, so that the rest also
will be fearful of sinning.
1 Timothy 5:19-20

The Bible does not tell us to refrain from correcting our elders. This is a misunderstanding that arises from 1 Tim 5:1 "rebuke not an elder." There is more harshness implied in "rebuke." The NIV, for example, says, "Do not rebuke an older man harshly." We should refrain from rebuking any Christian harshly. Paul gives special attention to situations where Timothy will have to correct older people.

The word "elder" can be understood in two correlations. One is an older person, as reflected in 5:2, where one should speak to an older woman as to a "mother." The other is someone who leads the church as an Elder. In the second case, we look to 1 Tim 5:19 NIV – "Do not entertain an accusation against an elder unless it is brought by two or three witnesses." Special care must be taken not to correct Christian leaders without grounds.

There does not seem to be any reason to limiting Paul's instructions. The verse is relevant for our interactions with either an Elder or to an older person. There is no reason in these verses to avoid correction of an older person because of his age or because of his office. There is no justification for what some church leaders do, erect a shield around them. Since a mere layperson should never "touch the Lord's anointed," they are permitted to do anything.

And you should imitate me,
just as I imitate Christ.
1 Corinthians 11:1 NLT

There are some who would even go as far to say, "Follow your leader whether they are right or wrong. When they go up, you will go up!" What happens if the leader goes down? You go down!

Moreover if thy brother shall trespass against thee, go and tell him his fault between thee and him alone: ... But if he will not hear [thee, then] take with thee one or two more ... And if he shall neglect to hear them, tell [it] unto the church: but if he neglect to hear the church, let him be unto thee as a heathen man and a publican.
Matthew 18:15-17

It seems that these Biblical passages are often overlooked. If a brother or sister rubs us the wrong way, we become enemies. We expect to go to heaven with our enemies.

Yet, we refuse to speak to these same people on earth. If we are facebook.com friends, we hit the defriend button. We forget that we are to love our enemies.

May the words of my mouth and the meditation
of my heart be pleasing to You, O LORD,
my rock and my redeemer.

Psalm   19:14   NLT

This prayer is familiar and used often. It is often prayed at the end of the church service. It should be prayed before we speak. Would you change the way you speak if you knew that every word and thought would be examined by God? Would you change your friends? Would you continue to lie? Would you let someone else choose your friends or enemies? Would you change the way that you live? David asks that God approve of his words and thoughts as though they were offerings brought to the altar. As you begin each day, determine that God's love will guide what you say and how you think. Determine that you will allow Him to guide your interactions with other people. Communicating with God allows Him to

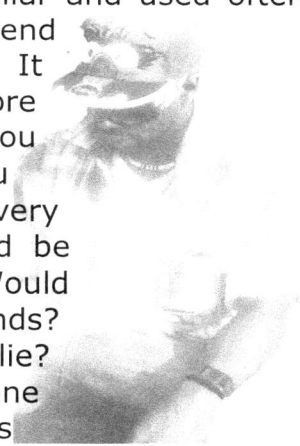

counsel, instruct, guide, rebuke, correct, and give us wisdom.

Better is a dish of vegetables where love is Than a fattened ox served with hatred.
Proverbs 15:17 NAS

The Biblical steps of correction are often omitted by leaders. The pulpits, the boardrooms, or courtrooms are their first point of correction. While personal lashes are being meted out to one, all are hit.

There is a huge difference between a sheep and a goat. There should always be a difference between Christians and nonbelievers. Sheep naturally have a loyalty to a good man of God who faithfully feeds them from the goodness of the Word of God.

An immature or ill-equipped shepherd (pastor) or a hireling finds it difficult to distinguish sheep and goats. Rather than feeding the sheep with sheep food, sheep are fed the goat's food. One of the marks of a goat is that it will eat almost anything. Much more than just eating it, it thinks that trash is delicious. The goats will feed themselves on what is popular, what is exciting, and what has little or no eternal value.

"If any man teach otherwise, and consent not to wholesome words... and to the doctrine which is according to godliness; he is proud, knowing

nothing but doting about questions and strifes of words... from such withdraw thyself."
1 Timothy 6:3-5

Sheep are particular about what they eat. When hungry sheep choke on this brittle food and begin to regurgitate, they are threatened with curses. When the hungry sheep go elsewhere looking for food seasoned with love, they are accused of church hopping. How many of our churches remain empty today because the hungry sheep were unable to thrive on goat's food?

And He shall set the sheep on His right hand but the goats on the left.
Matthew 25:31

The Good Shepherd, Jesus, knows the difference between sheep and goats. He easily separates them. He does not feed hungry sheep the food of goats. When a pastor follows this example, the sheep remain loyal because they are fed proper food.

Jesus received His harshest rebukes and criticism from the religious leaders. They were the ones always looking for fault in Him. They were always trying to trick or manipulate Him. They were the ones who demanded His execution. They had Him nailed to the cross. They didn't know that He was going to rise again. He continues to rise as each new convert gives Him the place of supreme authority in their life.

"Presumptuous are they, selfwilled, they are not afraid to speak evil of dignities. . . having eyes full of adultery, and that cannot cease from sin, beguiling unstable souls: an heart they have exercised with covetous practices ... they speak great swelling words of vanity . . . While they promise them liberty, they themselves are the servants of corruption: for of whom a man is overcome, of the same is he brought in bondage" 2 Peter 2:10-20

Leaders often want people to conform to their expectations. When this fails to happen, the person who refuses to conform may suffer religious persecution. Often, sermons are developed to bring them into conformity. These tactics are beneficial to some. But, when a person has acquired education or developed their ability to use deductive reasoning, these tactics are seldom effective.

Many churches would like to have members of their congregations who are professionals. People with education, financial stability, and social influence are seen as an enhancement to the ministry. Many of these same churches lack the basic ingredients that will attract these people to their churches. People who obtain this status seldom lack the ability to think analytically. These things will attract these people are:

- A sermon or message that is biblically sound.
- Opportunity for spiritual growth and enhancement.
- A sermon that is well prepared.
- Being treated with dignity and respect.
- Being shown love and support.
- Spiritual, financial, and ethical accountability from the leadership.

Is this what the Bible teaches us? Isn't this what Christ demands? Aren't these the instructions that Paul left Timothy? When these things are lacking, people eventually leave the church looking for a new one. Labeling them as church hoppers will not abort their search for these things.

The New Testament church went from house to house. In school, we seek educational advancement and promotion. On our jobs, we seek career advancement and promotion. This is expected and encouraged. Why is it that when we seek betterment in church experiences, this is viewed as a negative? When people begin to leave the church, why is there no internal quality review? Rather than looking internally for answers, they often ridicule or stigmatize those who left. An effective solution would be to identify and make the necessary corrections.

Behold, the days come, saith the Lord GOD, that I will send a famine in the land, not a famine of bread, nor a thirst for water but of hearing the words of the LORD.

Amos 8:11

Because of religious persecution, the saints took the gospel to other nations. It is because of religious persecution that there is a famine in the land today. This famine is not for meat or drink but for the Word of God. In recent years, I have met many people who have been hurt in the church. Sadly, after being hurt on numerous occasions, many of them are now seeking alternatives to traditional church services. We don't give up on the church because we are wounded. Although He had many problems with religious leaders, Jesus continued to go to church.

It is because of religious persecution within the church that many of God's children are wounded. Somebody, please get the oil! These wounds need a lot of oil poured into them.

If Virtuous Loses Virtue

The heart of her husband doth safely trust in
her, so that he shall have no need of spoil.
Proverbs 31:11

One morning, I woke up with this scripture on my mind. I began to think about it in a way that I never had before. What does this scripture mean to you? What does this scripture say to you? Recently, I posted this question on facebook.com. Here are few of the responses that I received.

La'Toya: I guess to me it means that a husband should be able to put his love and trust in his wife and know that she can hold it and that he won't have to worry about her hurting him or letting him down. I'm probably wrong but that's how I take it.

Carolyn: Charlotte, I think this scripture means that her husband can trust her and she will satisfy his every need. This would certainly be a very wonderful woman.

Charlotte Russell Johnson: OK men! Tell me what it means to you when you trust a woman with your heart!

Marquel Chill Gates Russell: This is a tough one, Cousin Charlotte Russell Johnson!

We as men love hard but don't show it much because of the fear of being hurt, so we keep our guard up. That's usually the reason for having multiple women. When we trust a woman with our heart, it is completely out of our comfort zone. I hope that makes sense.

Charlotte Russell Johnson: Marquel Chill Gates Russell, it makes a lot of sense.

Terina Monet': This scripture tells the role and responsibility of a woman. If a woman takes the responsibility of loving herself, taking care of herself, and simply cherishing her life altogether, then her husband or future husband will benefit from that because he will be able to trust her to love him, take care of him, and cherish their lives together. Women often blame men for doing them wrong and treating them badly. But often times, it is up to us to prove ourselves to be worthy of that true love from our husband or potential husband. Men become rotten after coming in contact with rotten women and vice versa. This scripture to me is telling women to take the responsibility of creating the marriage that they long for by earning the trust of their husband... but first, you need to do some self-evaluation. Am I trustworthy?

Madelyn: This one is a tough cookie. But to me, it means, that if the husband trusts in his woman, her decisions, and values that there would be no need for him to go out and please another especially since he has just what he needs in the one woman that he has. With him trusting her with his heart, thoughts of cheating should not cross his mind to the extent that she may cheat. There would be no need for him to go out and be greedy by getting all of the women that he can have. If there is a worry that another can take what's ours, it's apparent that it wasn't ours, to begin with! With God being the head of the relationship, everything else shall be added. With that being said, each person should live God first, self, then partner. You have to love them with the love of God thru it all. When the love is established, the trust comes soon afterward. In other words, you can't have one without the other. It's important that we take the precious gifts that God gives us (significant others) and take them in as if we never want to lose them and guard their feelings no matter the situation. But none of it can be possible without God.

Sonya Stewart: I had to read it for myself first. For me it is difficult to put in a few words but what I understand it to mean(for me) is that whatever the need is/in for the husband his wife holds, trust, honesty, honor, encouragement, loyalty, etc.

There is no need to look elsewhere, in the human sense. I will also add that the same should be said for the woman. I've always said that the woman is the backbone of her man. Meaning that whatever he needs from her, she has. I could relate this to "when a man finds a wife he finds a good thing". (May not be the exact quote but you know what I mean.

La'Toya: I don't know. It depends. You don't have to lay virtue aside. As long as you stay true to God and the Bible you will always be a virtuous woman. Yes, it's possible to lay your virtue aside but only if you lay God aside at the same time. God knows our hearts, and He knows our fates long before we do.

Terina Monet': Everybody makes mistakes but we all have the power to correct them. If you don't consider yourself a virtuous woman then strive to be it. You'll get there one day but like anything else it requires work. You just don't wake up one morning a virtuous woman. It's a process. Sometimes, you just simply have to be a girl.

Pamela H: To me, this means that in a marriage everything is blessed and the couple does not stray from GOD then all the attention from others will not faze them. If in your heart the attention is flattering somewhere look out cause the devil will be waiting. All the devil needs to know is if it gets just a little of your attention, and he will pounce.

Ronald S: That your wife is more precious than rubies, and a help mate.

In matters of love and relationships, men and women often have very different expectations. Therefore, I really wanted to understand this scripture from a man's point of view. Marquel really hit a home run by coming very close to what I needed to know.

Traditionally, men have been more adept at having long-term relationships that may have little to do with love. In many circles, this has been viewed as an acceptable behavior. It is more difficult for a man to commit his heart to a relationship. This is particularly true after his heart has been broken by a woman who lacks virtue.

Trends are changing. More women are becoming involved in relationships for the thrill. When a woman's heart is bruised and battered, she will often pick up the pieces and try again. Women can more easily trust someone with their heart. Men find this level of trust more difficult. When a man trusts a woman with his heart, it's a great sacrifice. He values his heart and he also his pride. He will not easily give either of them away.

Who can find a virtuous woman? for her
price *is* far above rubies.
Proverbs 31:10

What makes this virtuous woman so special? The man sees in her the characteristics that will allow him to trust one of his most valuable possessions with her, his heart. He trusts that she will never abuse that trust. She will never take for granted the gift that he has given her. She doesn't handle his heart and affection lightly.

The virtuous woman makes her man look good. She is careful of her appearance. She wants him to take pride in her. She is also careful of his reputation. She wants to be a valuable asset to her husband. Men call him blessed because she is so valuable. Men envy him and want this type of wife. He calls her blessed because she brings blessings to his life. Her children call her blessed because there are blessings that flow into their lives. She has principles and dignity. There are some things that she would never do. Her husband knows this truth. This is the reason he trusts her with his heart. He has no fear or doubt that she would mishandle his heart.

She will do him good and not evil all
the days of her life.
Proverbs 31:12

Is there ever a reason that a virtuous woman is free to hurt or harm her husband? The scripture says, "She will do him good **all the days of her life."** In times of anger, hurt, divorce, and trials spouses often do hurtful things. Hurt and wounded spouses often retaliate. Hurt people, hurt people. Wounded people, wound people.

Even in the best relationships, the opportunity or occasion for hurt will arise. Sometimes, it can appear that retaliation is justified. But is there an invisible line that should never be crossed? Some things would go beyond causing hurt or pain. They would cause deep wounds. For the virtuous woman, causing this type of pain is never an option. To do so would cause her to lose her virtue. Even when divorce or death has occurred, a virtuous woman respects her husband's memory and dignity.

Charm is deceptive, and beauty does not last; but a woman who fears the Lord will be greatly praised.
Proverbs 31:30 NLT

This woman is defined by more than her accomplishments. What does her husband, her servants, the poor and the needy, the community, and her children find unique about this woman? Her character shines! Are our relationships built on trust, generosity, dependability, and respect? Sometimes it may seem easier to work on our image rather than our relationships but God wants us to be involved in people's lives.

What is the priority of the woman of Proverbs? Fear of the Lord governs her life. This is a constructive fear that means acknowledging God's authority and allowing only God to order our lives. Some of us are people-pleasers, allowing the opinions of others to influence our choices. God's opinion of us is the only opinion that counts. God values us not because of what we accomplish but because of what He has accomplished for us in Jesus Christ. He wants to use this love and grace through us each day. A virtuous woman may cause hurt; she never wounds. The virtuous woman specializes in pouring oil into wounds.

Oil for the Divorced

"For I hate divorce!" says the Lord, the God of Israel. "To divorce your wife is to overwhelm her with cruelty," says the Lord of Heaven's Armies. "So guard your heart; do not be unfaithful to your wife."
Malachi 2:16

Divorce really hurts. Because the hurts run deep, it often leaves wounds. These wounds are hard to heal. Divorce hurts more than just the splitting partners. Tonsillitis, repeated ear infections, pneumonia, allergies, asthma, chronic skin conditions, chronic lung problems, and urinary infections are just some of the health problems reported among children of divorced parents. Low academic and social achievement is often encountered by children of divorced or separated parents.

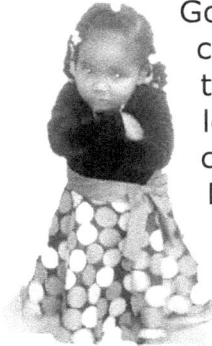

Gone is the myth that children can easily bounce back when their parents get a divorce. No longer do we believe the children will easily adjust. Divorce doesn't just affect the adults. These children are hurting too. They have wounds that need oil.

There are studies that

now confirm what Christians have always known. Christians have been insisting for decades that a loving family is the cornerstone of our society. This is not meant to suggest that marriages and homes will be healthy and happy simply because parents stay together. There are many situations where divorce is a more acceptable solution to ensure the health and safety of the children. Where there are abusive marriages and dysfunctional families, children also suffer.

When divorce occurs for Christians, it can leave them in a lost and lonely place. They aren't included in the singles' or the marriage ministry. Yet, they have ministry needs. Outreach towards this group is often lacking in the church.

Those who have endured a divorce are often seen as failures. When divorce occurs between Christians, the stigma is often more profound. Speculations and gossip often abound. Whose fault was it? Was there infidelity? Who failed to forgive? Will they get remarried? Are they free to remarry? Are they fit for leadership? This is hurtful and damaging. Yes, it causes deep wounds.

Divorce causes heartache. It brings this to each life it touches. Divorcees need the attention of their pastors and the members. Divorce is a growing problem and it often appears unavoidable. Divorce isn't going to go away by itself. Even if no one else divorces, our churches are filled with people who are affected by the devastation of divorce.

They need an understanding of how God now views them. They need to know how to respond to what God says about them. They need to know how to cope with or solve divorce-related problems.

Divorce is destructive. The effects reach beyond the two who are immediately involved. It affects the lives of children, parents, relatives, coworkers, social relationships, the church, future replacement partners and all these same individuals in all their area of influence. It has the potential to skew their outlook on life, relationships, the church, and God.

Many people who profess to be Christians play games with God by divorcing. They choose to divorce without biblical reasons and then act as if God didn't mind. They often continue to attend church and engage in "spiritual" activities or ministries. They may continue to serve in leadership roles thinking everything is fine. They look good on the outside. But read what God says about them:

You flood the Lord's altar with tears. You weep and wail because He no longer pays attention to

your offerings or accepts them with pleasure from your hands. You ask, "Why?" It is because the LORD is acting as the witness between you and the wife of your youth because you have broken faith with her, though she is your partner, the wife of your marriage covenant.
Malachi 2:13-14

When you divorce for unscriptural reasons, you drive a wedge between you and God, for you are rebelling against Him. It is rebellion against His Word. How is that person brought back into right relationship with God? But what happens to the party that is put away? Where does the person stand?

When we disobey God's Word, we suffer the consequences for our disobedience. When we honestly and humbly confess our sins, Christ helps us put the past behind and move forward. A wise pastor will not wink at or ignore these situations. He will seek godly wisdom to provide oil for these wounded partners.

God and God Alone

As the deer longs for streams of water, so I long
for You, O God. I thirst for God, the living God.
When can I go and stand before Him?
Psalm 42:1-2, NLT

As the life of a deer
depends on water, our
lives depend on our
relationship with God. He alone
is the source of our life and our
existence. Our relationship with
Him gives life true meaning.
Those who seek Him and long to
understand Him find the secret to
eternal life. Feeling separated
from God, this psalmist wouldn't
rest until his relationship with God
was restored. He knew that his life
depended on restoring this relationship.

God alone makes life meaningful
and worthwhile. If we put our complete trust
in anyone other than God, we are going to be
sadly disappointed. We are going to get hurt.
Sometimes, the hurt will be deep. It is just a
matter of time. Even the most devout saint
will disappoint you eventually.

Just as intimate relationships tend to
become unhealthy and dysfunctional when
partners demand too much or refuse to be

emotionally satisfied, so do relationships with spiritual leaders. No matter how much the other person gives, some people are never grateful. This includes time, loyalty, money, and devotion. The leader may withhold spiritual support or oust the person from the inner circle if all their demands aren't met. These demands often amount to Pharisaical legalism. The Bible has sat forth the qualifications for leaders. These biblical principles are often discarded for manmade rules. Just as the Pharisees did, these leaders impose rules and regulations that they are unwilling to keep themselves. Giving into these demands might seem to be the best way to gain spiritual acceptance or importance.

Regardless of the reason for staying in any relationship, dysfunctional relationships are costly. They rob you of your self-worth and self-appreciation. These relationships take lots of emotional and spiritual energy. Most people have been involved in some form of a dysfunctional relationship.

Where can we find the strength to confront the dysfunction? People can't give it to you! No amount of advice can change what is inside of you. How can Satan cast out Satan? These relationships often leave wounds that only God can pour oil into.

In a dysfunctional church, the pastor actually begins to take the place of Jesus in people's lives. Frequently, members are told they cannot leave the church with God's blessing unless the pastor approves of their decision. This implies that unless they receive permission from the pastor, not only will God not bless them but they will also be cursed in some way.

In a dysfunctional church, it is considered rebellion when members question the decisions made by leadership. Speeches that are made from the pulpit are considered as sacred law.

Still, there are those who constantly question the leadership in any church; often constant questioning comes from the individual's critical attitude. Pastors must learn to deal with questions in a compassionate and positive manner. In the dysfunctional church, any and all questions are considered a challenge to the pastor's "God-ordained" authority. Members who ask questions or who do not follow their pastor's directives are often confronted with severe consequences.

"They dress the wound of my people

as though it were not serious"
Jer. 8:11 NIV

When someone else assumes primary responsibility for another person's problems, the relationship is dysfunctional. When someone assumes that they have a better way of managing someone else's life, that relationship is also dysfunctional. When adults become overly invested in the lives of adults, the relationship is dysfunctional. When one person in a relationship feels a constant need to monitor the activities or behaviors of an adult, the relationship is dysfunctional.

"For God hath not given us the spirit of fear; but of power, and of love, and of a sound mind."
2 Timothy 1:7

Here are five obvious signs that a spirit of control is at work in a church:

1. Spiritual superiority. When a spirit of control is in a church, people are typically told that their group is unique. They believe they have special status with God. They presume to have exceptional revelation or favor. When members leave, they are rejected or labeled as having demons. In extreme cases, people are considered cursed if they leave. This cultic conduct causes inconceivable wounds and also divides

families and friends.

2. Limited or no accountability. The Bible says there is safety in the multitude of counselors. There is danger when a leader refuses to seek advice from a diverse group of their peers.

3. An oppressive atmosphere. Authoritarian leaders know how to control people through manipulation. In many cases, it may simply take the form of indirect innuendoes or advice. In the most abusive situations, it comes in the form of threats, legalism, harsh demands, excessive obligations, or false doctrines. In some churches, it comes during personal prophecies or mystic visions.

4. Individual guidance is discouraged. The Bible teaches that Christians have direct access to God through Christ Jesus. He is the only mediator between God and man.

5. Angry domination and demonstrations. Dictators are surprisingly similar. They have many similar traits. Because they want total control, they will bash people who refuse to conform to their demands. Anger always accompanies a controlling spirit.

"It was for freedom that Christ set us free; therefore keep standing firm and do not be subject again to a yoke of slavery."
Galatians 5:1 NASB

Some leaders teach their congregations to seek approval from the pastor before making all major decisions. In some extreme cases, they also consult the pastor for minor decisions. Thus church members develop an unhealthy dependence on a man or woman in order to function spiritually. Their ability to trust God is minimal.

Many who submit to this belief will require years to recover from the loss of their decision-making ability. After forfeiting their wills and losing their self-identity, they trust their leader more than God. They view absolute obedience to their spiritual leaders as a Christian virtue.

In making these statements, I am referring to adults managing the life of an adult who is not physically, emotionally, socially, or psychologically impaired, or challenged. Those who are challenged in these areas may need assistance.

If you are not challenged in these areas, stand up! Take your life back and give it to the person who can be trusted to lead you and guide you into all truths. Allow God to heal the dysfunctions. Give Him complete control. His motives are not selfish or based on His dysfunctions. He has none! Allow Him to pour oil into your wounds.

Oil for the Married

The man who finds a wife finds a treasure and
receives favor from the LORD
Proverbs 18:22

Marriage is hard work. It should never be entered into lightly. Spiritual counseling is a necessity for Christian couples considering marriage. Before choosing a counselor, it is wise to consult the all WISE counselor. A counselor who lacks the appropriate spiritual and natural qualifications can hinder marriage preparedness.

How do you choose the right counselor? This choice requires a lot of prayers. Your pastor may or may not be the person to provide this counseling. A pastor who is unmarried or who has gone through a painful divorce may lack the objectivity to effectively counsel. If the pastor is married, observing their relationship with their spouse may give indications. Are biblical principles being applied in their relationship? Is there balance in the relationship?

If the pastor is willing to discuss your spouse without them being present, this may be an indication that the pastor lacks the professionalism to conduct marriage counseling. If the pastor provides personal opinions rather than biblical advice, this is another warning sign. If it appears that the pastor sides with one partner rather than seeking a win/win solution, this is another indicator. *If it were me* is a definite indicator. When they express these thoughts, you need to run. It's not them; this is your life. You will have to live with the outcome. EVERY counseling session should begin and end with prayer. When it is inadvisable to pray aloud, silent prayer is always possible. Lives are at stake. God alone has the answers. His intervention and guidance is a must.

Marriage is called the *acid test of discipleship* because the people at home know you. People can put up a front at church or in other surroundings. At home, the truth will be known. Marriage problems are discipleship problem. They often arise because one or both partners refuse to obey the scriptures.

Spiritual intimacy can be acquired by studying scripture together, praying, sharing beliefs, and building each other up in the Lord. These things are not possible with a non-believer. This is why the Bible warns us about being yoked with unbelievers.

If the marriage is going to thrive, each person has to take responsibility for their actions. There are many wounds that can occur in marriage. A well-prepared counselor will be able to pour oil on these wounds.

Prelude to a Drama

For where envying and strife is, there is
confusion and every evil work.
James 3:16

On the first Sunday morning that I
began attending a new church, the pastor
asked me to join this church. This church has
great plans. It has the potential to be used
for God's glory. Additionally, many talented
entertainers attend this ministry. Out of my
love and concern for the people, I will not
identify this ministry. They have publicly and
openly identified themselves on the social
media, facebook.com.

He said, "Listen, all you people of Judah and
Jerusalem! Listen, King Jehoshaphat! This is
what the LORD says: Do not be afraid! Don't be
discouraged by this mighty army,
for the battle is not yours but God's."
2 Chronicles 20:15 NLT

We may not fight an enemy army but
every day we battle temptation, criticism,
lies, ungodliness, selfishness, pride,
pressure, and many other things designed to
make us turn away from God. Satan's
ultimate goal is to get us to rebel against
God. Remember, as believers in Christ, we

have God's Spirit within us. If we ask for God's help when we face our trials, God will fight our battles for us. God always triumphs over the enemy.

The LORD is my rock, my fortress, and my savior; my God is my rock, in whom I find protection. He is my shield, the power that saves me, and my place of safety. I called on the LORD, who is worthy of praise, and He saved me from my enemies.
Psalm 18:2-3 NLT

God's protection of His people is not bound by restraints. It is limitless and can take many forms. David characterized God's care with five military symbols. God is a rock that can't be moved by any who try to harm us. He's a fortress, a place of safety where the enemy can't follow us. He's a shield that comes between us and harm. He is a horn of salvation, a symbol of might and power. He's a stronghold high above our enemies. When you need protection, look to God.

I accept all blame in this matter, my lord.
1 Samuel 25:24 NLT

Abigail serves as a valuable role model to all who desire to serve God with honor under difficult conditions. In keeping with her example, I take full responsibility for my decision to join this church. It appeared to be a good thing. Therefore, I acted on impulse. It is always wise to pray. Even what appears to be a good thing for the right reason can be a very wrong thing. If there had been a win/win option in this situation, I would have opted for that solution. There wasn't one.

I love them but they try to destroy me with accusations even as I am praying for them!
Psalm 109:4 NLT

David was angry at being attacked by evil people who slandered his name and lied about him. Indeed, this can be painful. David remained a friend to his enemies. As a man of prayer, he continued to pray for them. We have to keep this same attitude.

While we are to hate evil and work to overcome it, we must also love our enemies. This includes those who do evil because God loves them. We are called to hate the sin but not the sinner. It is only through God's strength that we can follow David's example.

Give thanks to the LORD, for He is good! His faithful love endures forever. Has the LORD redeemed you? Then speak out! Tell others He has redeemed you from your enemies.
Psalm 107:1-2 NLT

The pastor and a number of members of the church launched an attack on my character and reputation. They did this primarily through facebook.com. Because of the depth of the wound, I chose not to respond at that time. Even now, I will not provide the details of this experience in their entirety. Nor will I identify the church or the parties involved. Because their comments were posted in a public forum, I have a legal right to do so. Although they extended no grace towards me in this matter, I bare them no malice. In telling this, I will extend grace towards all parties directly involved.

When there are many words, transgression is unavoidable but he who restrains his lips is wise.
Proverbs 10:19 NAS

When I joined Thespian Church where Bishop Ayo Aines is the pastor, Joe had already been attending there for a several months. Unbeknown to me, two young women at the church had been actively pursuing relationships with him. Although the relationship with one of the women, Airel, never went beyond flirtation, a storm was brewing. The relationship with the other young woman, Pseuda, began to develop.

But the LORD's plans stand firm forever; His

intentions can never be shaken.
Psalm 33:11 NLT

The plans of the LORD stand firm forever. Our plans may waver and shake but His plans never change. He is a sure foundation. He is completely trustworthy! His intentions towards His children never change. There is a promise that every good and perfect gift comes from above. He is never fickle. Let Him counsel you; trust His plans for your life.

How can a young person stay pure? By obeying Your word and following its rules.
Psalm 119:9 NLT

All around us, we find temptations to lead impure lives. How do we stay pure in a perverted society? We cannot do this on our own but must have counsel and strength more powerful than the tempting influences around us. Where can we find the strength and wisdom to stand? By reading God's Word and doing what it says. Commitment to God is a sustainer. HE is a "Keeper".

One night, Joe walked into my bedroom. I had already retired for the night. It was after midnight. He was pacing back and forth; this was his way of awakening me. It was also my clue that something was wrong.

While I had become suspicious that something was cooking between him and Pseuda, I had no proof. When I asked him what was wrong, he explained that a minister from the church had called to strongly warn him not to become involved with Pseuda. Unaware that Joe was riding with Pseuda, the minister explained his position. Pseuda overheard the conversation. Joe had the speakerphone on. He did this so Pseuda would know that he wasn't talking negatively about her. However; he didn't know the extent that the minister was going to discuss her and her past.

As Joe was telling me this, Pseuda called him. The cell phone enabled me to hear all the negative things that she was saying about herself. In an effort to comfort her and bring peace, I asked Joe to give me the cell phone and leave the room.

My interactions with Pseuda had always been positive. She had encouraged me to join the church. When Joe left the room, I asked Pseuda to stop speaking negatively about herself. Afterward, I asked her if she liked Joe.

Pseuda responded, "Yes, I like him but I am just…"

Before she finished the negative tirade, I cut her off, "If you like him, don't sleep with him. You will never have a meaningful relationship with him if you do. He's looking for somebody who will say, 'No!'"

We talked on for a while after this. During that time I tried to give her some advice to keep herself from falling into sexual immorality.

Stepping out of the role of a mother, I stepped into the role of Christian counselor and evangelist, "You need to cover each other in prayer. Avoid tempting situations. Avoid spending time alone. If the urge arises, start speaking in tongues."

Later that night, I saw Pseuda at church. Her eyes were red and watery. She told me that she had confessed everything to the pastor. Afterward, I told Joe that he should expect the pastor to counsel him. He was already expecting this to occur.

The following Monday, we were at a leadership meeting. Sex was the topic or the focus of the discussion. It was a regular topic of discussion. At the time, I didn't know it.

Ignorantly, I stated, "Some people are obsessed with thoughts of other people having sex because they aren't having sex."

Bishop Ayo Aines retorted, "People come to you to tell you about their sexual affairs because they are out of order. They know you have that same 'hoe' spirit and you will be soft on them. You are out of order too or you would point them back to their pastor."

Rather than taking full offense at her remarks, I tried to assume that her remarks were not directed towards me. I reasoned: Surely, she isn't referring to me. It has only been a month or so since I started attending here; maybe, I'm over sensitive. It's just that I don't know her well. This was the way that I rationalized it.

Oh, the joys of those who do not follow the advice of the wicked, or stand around with sinners, or join in with mockers.
Psalm 1:1 NLT

This Psalm begins extolling the joys of obeying God. We should refuse to listen to those who discredit, contradict, or ridicule His wisdom and His word. Our friends and associates can have a profound influence on us. This influence is often in very subtle ways. When we insist on friendships with those who mock what God considers important, we are tempted to fall into sin by becoming indifferent to God's will. This attitude is the same as mocking.

Do your friends build up your faith, or do they tear it down? A true friend should help you to draw closer to God. They should not hinder your relationship with Him.

One day, I noticed that Joe's spirit was vexed. When I enquired about this, he denied that anything was wrong. As a concerned and overprotective mother, he didn't fool me. Since his relationship with Christ had recently been renewed, I did not want anything or anyone to discourage him. I continued watching him, trying to figure it out.

A couple of days later, I was dropping him off at the church. By this time, I was convinced that one of the ministers at the church had something to do with his disposition. Elder Minni was at the church when we arrived. Rather than driving off, I went inside of the church to her office.

After the initial chit-chat, I asked, "What is going on between you and Joe?"

She began to make justification, "You see, Bishop talked to them."

Not willing to be swayed, I interrupted, "I'm not referring to Bishop. As the pastor of this church, he was expecting her to counsel them. I am only referring to your interaction with him."

Let no unwholesome word proceed from your mouth but only such a word as is good for edification according to the need of the moment, so that it will give grace to those who hear.
Ephesians 4:29 NAS

Elder Minni's response shocked me, "The only thing that I am concerned with is

Airel! She lives in my house! She got a hoe (whoreish) spirit! I'm not going to have that hoe spirit up in my house! I told Brother Joe that she got a hoe spirit! If she gon' start dating, she needs to move out my house and let her boyfriend take care of her."

This was not exactly what I was expecting. It is my nature to teach subtlety whenever the opportunity presents itself. Very gently, I said, "Did you enquire of their relationship with God? Did you ask if there has been repentance?"

She continued, "Bishop gave me permission to talk to Brother Joe. I tell Bishop everything! She knew exactly what I was gon' say! When Brother Joe came here, I tried to warn him that a lot of women over here were going to try to get with him! He's not thinking about either one of them! He's just using both of them! But that hoe spirit is not going to stay in my house!"

Again I repeated, "Did you enquire of their relationship with God? Did you ask if there has been repentance? How is Joe using them? He has only flirted with Airel and he has feelings for Pseuda. What is he using them for?"

Elder Minni was adamant, "I knowed all this was gon' happen. God warned me that it was not going to go well before I talked to him! I'm not concerned about all that! I just don't want that hoe spirit in my house! I told him if I catch her smiling and grinning in his face one more time, she has to get out of my house! She just a hoe! Bishop gave me permission to say everything that I said! I knowed this was gon' happen!"

When I left there, all I could do was shake my head. When counseling anyone, as Christians, our objective should always be restoration. If our motive is not to restore the person to right relationship with God, He has not led us to have the interaction. When God gives us instructions, He has directions to accompany the instructions.

While Joe had no real romantic intentions in Airel, he felt sorry for her. He was hurt that she was living under these conditions. He was sorry that she was referred to by this name. He was even sorrier when he learned the reason for the name.

It wasn't long before the pastor used the same term in the same context in Bible study. When referring to sexual liaisons outside of marriage, she yelled, "You're just a hoe!" On another occasion, she referred to people as being "faggots." She said that she was teaching hard. To me, it was just crude and graphic. For more than thirty years, I have been under the influence of the teachings of the Pentecostal church. The teachings of *Holiness or Hell* have been a staple of my diet; I have never heard anything close to the teachings of this church.

Numerous efforts from people within the church, including the pastor, were made to discourage Joe's interest in Pseuda. The most intimate and personal details of her life were shared with him. Many things about her were later shared with me. During numerous Bible studies, the information shared was directly from pages of her life. Each time an incident happened between Pseuda and Joe, information related to her life was shared openly.

My heart was grieved. The sin was bad enough. The way it was carelessly shared and discussed grieved me more. Pseuda and Joe loved and respected this pastor. Pseuda would probably give her life for her. But, I watched Pseuda's face as her life and pain were put on display. It tore at my heart. Pseuda has many issues. She needs to be delivered. Insults and embarrassments have failed to provide the healing that she needs.

Other leaders within the church shared information about Pseuda. It was common knowledge around the church that this person slept with that one. This one wouldn't sleep with this one. This one did this to that one. All the different talk about sex kept the spirit of perversion alive. It kept many of their sexual imagination stirred and active.

If you are trying to stop drinking alcohol, don't hang around people who continuously talk about drinking. If you are trying to remain sexually pure, don't call into a sex hotline. Don't tune into a Bible study where vivid sexual pictures are painted. It will pour something into the wound but it's not oil.

As it is my nature to empathize with the underdog, so I did with Pseuda. Because of her plight in life, I was saddened that those she had trusted with this information would use it against her. Rather than judging or belittling her, I prayed for emotional healing for her and her family. Judging her family was not an option. I began to intercede on their behalf. My desire was that they would have oil for their wounds.

After hearing these things about her, it would be extremely difficult for any mother to choose her as a companion for their son. What mother does not want the best for her child? Although many of these things were troubling, I attempted to accept Joe's choices. Nevertheless, I shared my concerns with him. Her present behavior concerned me more than her past behavior.

Our children will also serve Him. Future generations will hear about the wonders of the

Lord. His righteous acts will be told to those not yet born. They will hear about everything He has done.

Psalm 22:30-31 NLT

If we want our children to serve the Lord, they must hear about Him from us. We must also teach them the Biblical qualities that are found in godly mates and the importance of selecting godly companions. It is not enough to rely on the church or those with more knowledge to provide their Christian education. We must reinforce the lessons of the Bible in our homes.

My first desire for my children is that their spouses be saved, sanctified, and full of the Holy Spirit. My second desire is that God would reign supreme in the lives of their spouses. My third desire is that their spouses would be an asset to their walk with Christ. I want them to be equally yoked with their spouses. It is my heart's desire that my children will also be that kind of mate. This has always been my prayer for my children. My prayer has not changed or wavered.

Call me old-fashioned if you must but when my children marry, their spouses will be accepted as members of our immediate family. They will be given the same the rights and privileges afforded my children. My children are close and they each desire to see the other happy. They are also protective of each other.

Although Joe never made his relationship with Pseuda official, she was very bold. She informed me that when Joe married, the closeness between us would have to cease. She further informed me that if it did not, I would be violating the Bible by not allowing him to cleave to his wife. There were many things that I wanted to say to Pseuda. Rather than saying them to her, I remained nice; I said them to Joe.

After carrying Joe inside my body for nine months, enduring twenty-three hours of hard labor, standing by him through countless tragedies, and nurturing his relationship with God, I will always be close to him. Joe has been trained to treat all women with dignity and respect. He has heard countless lectures on the value of being a good provider for his family, a supportive and nurturing father, a faithful and true husband, and assuming his responsibilities as the head of his family. If he treats his family in any other way, it would break my heart. Nonetheless, Pseuda was pushing too hard.

Since I know God hears my prayers, I have not only prayed for my children but I have also prayed for any future spouses. My prayer requests have been very specific.

They have not been selfish prayers. With confident assurance, I patiently wait in expectation for the answer to my prayers. Having my prayers answered sooner is not an option if the request has to be lessened.

May the Lord grant that each of you will find rest in the home of another husband." Then she kissed them goodbye and they wept aloud.
Ruth 1:9

Ruth was poor, a foreigner, and a woman, and all this counted against her. She was helped by her mother-in-law, Naomi, to overcome the difficulties she faced. In return, Naomi was rewarded by Ruth's unfaltering loyalty. Her story illustrates the triumph of courage and ingenuity over adverse circumstances. The story of Ruth and Naomi is a very powerful story. Every mother-in-law should love her daughter-in-law the way Naomi loved both of hers. Every daughter-in-law should have the loyalty of Ruth towards her mother-in-law.

Shortly after Pseuda made it known to me that she planned to marry Joe, the church took a trip to Macon, GA. After the service, Pseuda was walking ahead of me down a hall. I needed assistance. As Christians, when people need minimal or basic help, it is our duty to assist them. Opening doors and speaking are basic courtesies.

Since she failed to help me, I said jokingly to her, "If you are going to be my Ruth, you will have to look out for me."

To my surprise, she responded, "My bishop is my everything!"

Since the relationship between Ruth and Naomi is predefined, I responded, "You need to marry her son then."

Although my original comment was meant lightly, the conversation revealed a lot of truth. It is not possible for Joe to be her husband or for her to be my daughter-in-law if her pastor is fulfilling these roles. Her answer sounded strange to me but I accepted this. How can one person be everything to you? Spouses or lovers often express these sentiments. Where does this leave Jesus? Just as Naomi had encouraged her daughter-in-laws to find other husbands, I encouraged Pseuda to do the same.

When it comes to Joe, I would prefer that his wife is untainted. Truthfully, Joe introduced me to the woman I wanted him to marry, years ago. At that time, he needed to mature. She deserved and still deserved the best from her mate. She is a special young Christian woman. My immediate family was praying for that situation to work out. Because of Joe's procrastination, it didn't.

There are many other things that **I** would prefer for Joe. Still, it is God's job to select his wife. Pseuda does not meet my specifications. There is no need for me to elaborate further. I have no desire to tear her down or berate her. Throughout this ordeal, I have been careful not to do that.

It was my desire to see Pseuda strengthened in her walk with the Lord. There were enough people stepping on her; she didn't need me to add to it. Nevertheless, this is what she has grown accustomed to. She misunderstood my kindness towards her. God has shown me mercy and grace. This is what I extended to her. If God was willing to embrace her, why should I do otherwise?

O LORD, You have searched me and known me. You know when I sit down and when I rise up; You understand my thought from afar. You scrutinize my path and my lying down, And are intimately acquainted with all my ways.

Psalm 139:1-3 NAS

Throughout my life, I have sought to help others in need. During my Christian journey, I have given unselfishly of my time, talents, skills, ability, and finances to assist others in obtaining a better quality of life. If I had chosen to deal with Pseuda in any other way, it would have made my life's work null and void.

She has not brought any positive benefits to my life, nor do I see the potential of her doing so. She had neither spiritual, financial, or social assets to benefit my life. This has never been my expectation of her or anyone else. God is my provider and the source of my strength. He has never come short in either of these roles. He is also my sustainer.

But I keep praying to You, LORD, hoping this time You will show me favor. In Your unfailing love, O God, answer my prayer with Your sure salvation.
Psalm 69:13 NLT

King David faced numerous problems. His own son led a rebellion and uprising against him. Another son raped David's daughter. He was scoffed at, mocked, insulted, humiliated, and made the object of city-wide gossip. But still, David prayed. His faith never wavered. When we are completely beaten down, it can be tempting to turn from God. When the situation seems hopeless, determine that no matter how bad things become you will continue to pray. When others reject us, we need God most. Don't turn from your most faithful friend.

Do our prayers end with requests for help to make it through stressful situations? David prayed not merely for rescue but for victory. He prayed for victory over his enemies. With God's help, we can claim more than mere survival, we to can claim victory!

He will rescue the poor when they cry to Him; He will help the oppressed, who have no one to defend them. He feels pity for the weak and the needy, and He will rescue them. He will redeem them from oppression and violence, for their lives are precious to Him.
Psalm 72:12-14 NLT

God cares for the needy, the rejected, the outcast, the afflicted, and the weak because they are precious to Him. If God feels so strongly about these needy ones and loves them so deeply, how can we ignore their plight? He wants us to care for those in need. How could I refuse to reach out to Pseuda with God's love? Are you ignoring their plight of the needy and fragile or are you meeting their needs?

Sadly, there are many people who have never experienced unconditional love. They are accustomed to being used and abused. They accept this as something that they deserve. They feel unlovable because they believe the lies that Satan has fed them. They only understand selfish love. But doesn't the Bible teach us that love is unselfish?

The LORD is like a father to His children, tender and compassionate to those who fear Him. For He knows how weak we are; He remembers we are only dust.
Psalm 103:13-14 NLT

We are fragile jars of clay but God's care is eternal. We often focus on God as judge and lawgiver, ignoring His compassion and concern. When God examines our lives, He remembers our human condition. Yet, our weakness does not serve as justification for sin. God's mercy takes everything into account. God will deal with you compassionately. Trust in Him because He cares for you.

To be fair to Pseuda, I did observe some positive impact that she had upon Joe. Yet, she destroyed everything that she accomplished. She did not destroy what God has accomplished. Although Pseuda warned me repeatedly that one day I would hate her, I do not hate her. My prayer is simply for God to forgive her for what she has done. We have forgiven her misguided deeds. We did not allow anyone to pour salt in this wound. The oil continuously flowed throughout this process. Immediately after I completed my last book, God began to deal with me about this book. It happened so quickly that I found it surprising. As He was dealing with me about the importance of recovering from wounds, the wounds began to come. They were all related to the church. This was just one more in the series. It was a necessary hurt to complete this book. This is the way I think about the things that happened. It was oil poured into my wounds. As for Joe, Joe, he has found his own oil. This oil has been his sustainer for many years. He found healing for his wounds in the Word of God!

I do Love U!

My child, never forget the things I have taught
you. Store my commands in your heart.
Proverbs 3:1

When a child suffers emotional trauma,
they often develop post-traumatic stress
disorder. The symptoms are very similar to
those experienced by military servicemen
after serving in a war. Indeed, many of our
children are raised in war zones, their
homes. On more than one occasion, I have
attempted to help someone with this
disorder. They have deep hurts. They have
deep wounds. They need oil for their
wounds.

The past failures of those who should
have provided this oil will cause them to
distrust anyone who appears to care about
them. They often reject the oil that
they desperately need and crave.
They often hurt the Good
Samaritan.

There is a young woman
very dear to my heart. She
suffered from this disorder.
Throughout her life, I attempted to
pour oil on her wounds. On
numerous occasions, she knocked
the oil away. There were others

who tried. She responded the same way. This was her way of protecting her heart. Shelena died several years ago. Whether the oil ever reached the wound, I don't know. It is a source of regret for me. Recently, I was reminded that my heart still grieves for this young woman. In many ways, she was my child.

But thanks be to God, which giveth us the victory
through our Lord Jesus Christ.
1 Corinthians 15:57

The young woman that Joe became involved with, Pseuda had many things in common with Shelena. Their histories and backgrounds are amazingly similar. Perhaps, I viewed her as another opportunity to rescue Shelena. When Shelena passed she chose to slip away from me without saying goodbye. This is a wound that I need oil poured into. Over the years, Shelena shared so many of her painful life experiences with me. During many of these, I walked through the valley with her.

As I am writing this, my eyes began to fill with tears. The pain of Shelena's loss became alive. What an awesome God I serve! He decided to pour oil into my wound. He reminded me of a letter that Shelena wrote me in 2000. Although I hadn't seen it in years, I was sure that I still had it. With very little effort, I found it. I'll share a portion of it below. Shelena was not her real

name. Her name was Shelena.

11-27-2000

Dear Charlotte,

Time plus the pleasure has allowed me the opportunity to drop you these few lines... I am blessed that the Lord has allowed me to see another day.

I must say that it was more than a pleasure to hear from you. God always send you when I need you the most. Always every time. You are my personal angel and I thank God for you.

Today they called me out to see the doctor and the news was not good... He believes I need to change meds. That the ones I have been taking are no longer working. So I was pretty upset and scared. But when I received the message you sent, I began to regroup and call on the Lord putting my life and health in His hands. With Him, I know I can make it.

Thanks for always being there for me. Never giving up on me.

Since I ..., I've been writing poems. Yes, I make them up word for word on my own. Here is one that I wrote just for you today.

I do love u!
As time presses on and things start to change,
I have changed too, thanks to you.
I have done things to you may never forget the
hurt and the pain that I have caused you and the
sadness in your eyes, all due to my ugly ways and
lies; how is it that you do not despise me but
continue to care, loving me beyond the compare.
How I look at these things.
Suddenly a bell starts to ring inside my head
letting me know I have been a fool.
So all I ask of you is to forgive me please and
never let me go because I do love you.

Keep me in your prayers.

Much love and respect,
Shelena

"LORD, remind me how brief my time on earth
will be. Remind me that my days are numbered--

how fleeting my life is."
Psalm 39:4 NLT

Life is short no matter how long we live. If there is something important we want to do, we should not put it off for a better day. Ask yourself, "If I had only six months to live, what would I do?"

That was a question that I was given as a topic for the Regent's Exam. A portion of the exam is an essay that determines your preparedness to graduate from college. It was easy for me to answer that question. It is a question worth pondering. Would you tell someone that you loved them? Repent of some sin? Deal with an undisciplined area in your life? Get closer to God? Tell someone about Jesus Christ? Because life is too short, don't neglect the things that are truly important.

Almost four years later, July 24, 2004, Shelena left me. During this time, I have lived with regret because I thought I failed her. I wanted desperately to pour oil into her wounds. Because I wasn't there when she slipped away, I thought I had failed. My loving God has reminded me of what I already knew. When I got this letter I knew my efforts had not been wasted. My grief caused me to forget. Oil was poured into Shelena's wounds.

My darling Shelena, I never held the pain of what you did. My love for you was unconditional. It was that love that has allowed me to love so many other Shelenas. It is the kind of love that I extended to this young woman that Joe was involved with, Pseuda. When I told Pseuda that I would never hate her, she couldn't understand the statement. My history with Shelena assured me that I would be unable to hate Pseuda. I understood her, too well. Shelena gave me a good education.

Behold, I show you a mystery; We shall not all sleep but we shall all be changed,
1 Corinthians 15:51

When Shelena passed, depression became my constant companion. Guilt made her death extremely hard to bear. On more than one occasion, we were faced with the possibility of her impending demise. Each time, I went through it with her. Over the years, I have been with several people as they transcended this life. It was just assumed that I would be there for her.

When I received a call that she was in the hospital and appeared to be nearing the end, I tried to prepare myself. When I called the hospital, I was expecting her to be in intensive care. Instead, she answered the phone in her room. She made light of her condition. Because I was going through a personal tragedy, I accepted her explanation. Perhaps, she just didn't want to tell me the truth over the telephone.

Two days later, I went to the hospital. Prior to going inside, I called the hospital to verify her room number. I was told that she had been discharged. Assuming she had bounced back as in times past, I didn't attempt to locate her. No matter how many times in the past our assumptions have been right, there will be times when our assumptions are wrong.

Whenever Shelena needed me, she always called. That was the way that it happened in times past. This time, the call never came. In the past, this had always meant that she didn't need me. It wasn't until she passed that I learned she had been transferred to a local hospice. Why didn't she tell me the end was near? Maybe she didn't want to tell me over the telephone. I just don't know!

"The LORD is my strength and my shield; My
heart trusts in Him, and I am helped;
Therefore my heart exults, And with
Song I shall thank Him."
Psalm 28:7 NAS

Each situation is unique and should be

treated as such. What works extremely well to ease the pain of one person may have little effect on the pain of another. Sensitivity, grace, love, and mercy are necessary for every situation. Because we have been healed of our wounds, we will have the potential to aid others by pouring oil into their wounds. It behooves us to be sensitive to opportunities to promote healing.

My choice is to grow from each adversity that comes in my life. As we learn the lessons from our wounds, we are free to move forward. When we accept totally and completely God's plans for our life, God can move us forward. Forgiveness is an option. Over the years, the pain of Shelena's loss has gotten better. The guilt and the what-ifs remained. Learning to forgive ourselves for some perceived failure is part of the healing process. The healing has begun. Forgiveness pours oil into the wound.

Dear God, I pray for Your children everywhere who are wounded in ways that seem beyond repair. Heal them now for Your glory! Restore to them the joy of their salvation!

Touching and Agreeing

For He issued His laws to Jacob; He gave His instructions to Israel. He commanded our ancestors to teach them to their children

Psalm 78:5 NLT

God commanded that the stories of His mighty acts and deeds be passed on from parents to the children. This shows the purpose and importance of religious education. This is to help each generation obey God and set their hope on Him. My children have had formal Christian education. They were raised on a solid diet of wholesome spiritual food. They know the difference between good and evil. They also know the difference between right and wrong. Should they make the wrong decision, it is not because they weren't taught. It is extremely important to keep children from repeating the same mistakes as their ancestors. I have instilled this truth in them.

Joe is free to choose his friends and relationships. Indeed, he has always done so. I have not always approved of his choices or his friends. Over the years, I have learned to accept his right to choose; this has not stopped me from expressing my disapproval.

For some reason, Joe was not

dismayed by the things that he was told about her. Pseuda had already shared the information with him. My only concerns were that they not date secretly or have premarital sex. These concerns were shared with both of them.

Drink water from your own well—
share your love only with your wife.
Proverbs 5:15 NLT

We should be helping our young people learn how to make the right choices and how to do what is right. This responsibility includes teaching them how to have the courage to say NO. It can be difficult to control sexual desires in a society that overrates sex. The church should not contribute to these thoughts. Every message in the church should not include vivid references to sexual gratification. Adding in raging hormones and permissive adults, and there's a volatile mix.

There is a way to discuss sex that is appropriate and a way that is inappropriate. There is a way to counsel people who fall into error or sin. There is a way that is inappropriate. Across the pulpit is never appropriate for individual sexual counseling.

One day, Pseuda and Joe were at another church. They made plans to spend time together later. Joe had someone drop him off at a nearby restaurant. She picked him up from there. They stopped at a grocery store to pick up some items for dinner. Shortly after they arrived at Pseuda's apartment, they discovered that Minister Jack had followed them. The minister reported this information to Bishop Aines. She instantly called to speak to Pseuda. They talked for a couple of minutes. Minister Jack asked Joe to leave with him. Joe asked to be dropped off at a nearby restaurant. When they got there, Minister Jack warned Joe about Pseuda.

Minister Jack adamantly stated, "You shouldn't date her. Look at her! You know that you don't want to marry her. She's a disgrace to the ministry. Any man who puts his hand to the plow and takes it back is not worthy to live; so, she's not worthy to live right now. She knows better! This is not the first time that this has happened! Don't think that if she is…that you are the only one. She is not that kind of girl. I'll say it to her face! You just don't know what kind of trouble you got yourself into! Did you know that her mom is a… and her dad is a… Do you know what kind of spirits you just allowed to connect to you? Now, your soul is connected to a demonic spirit!"

Joe interrupted him, "No! It's not! No, I'm not connected to a demonic spirit! No disrespect minister but I'm not interested in you telling me all of her past and her parents past history. Thanks for trying to warn me. However, she has already told me everything that you are trying to tell me. As a friend or brother if you know something about her personal life, that doesn't mean you should just go around telling people. What if she hadn't already told me?! No offense, thanks for the advice but I can make my own decisions about being with her."

Minister Jack began to share his personal sexual deviances. He again tried to persuade Joe that Pseuda was not the type of woman who he wanted to marry.

Refusing to give up, Minister Jack asked, "Do you like her? Do you want to marry her? Do you love her?"

To the continuous onslaught of questions, Joe answered, "Yes! I like her. I love her! I am not trying to marry anyone at this time; I'm trying to get myself together."

Refusing to give up, Minister Jack pressed, "Joe look at her. Can you see yourself married to someone like that for the rest of your life? Man, you know that you don't want to marry that girl."

One night after a Bible study that was particularly vulgar and graphic, Joe and I were invited out to eat at a nearby restaurant by a member of the church. We agreed to meet him. When we arrived, he said that he was expecting a third person. We assumed that he was referring to his girlfriend. After we had been there for some time, Minister Jack walked in. We waved to him. He walked over to the table and told the man that Pseuda would not be coming. When he walked out, Joe dropped his head.

Shaking his head, Joe said, "Here we go again."

Prior to this time, the man that we were dining with had no knowledge of Joe's relationship with Pseuda. He had observed him talking to numerous women but not this one. Needless to say, the man was shocked. In no way was he attempting to be a matchmaker.

While we were at the restaurant, Joe attempted to call Pseuda but she didn't answer her cell phone. A short time later, she called my cell phone. She wanted to know if she could meet me and Joe at the house. Expecting unavoidable drama, I agreed.

Pseuda came to my home. She stated that she came to break off her relationship with Joe and to apologize to me for the damage that she had done. She was also there to convince me to remain at the church. Her words served the opposite purpose. They served to confirm my concerns about the ministry. I listened to her passionate recital.

With great drama and flair, she stated, "I've got to break this off! You don't understand; it's not God's will for my life. I know you think it's my bishop but it's not. I have good leaders. It's me! It's me! I'm just so manipulative! I caused all this! I manipulated this whole situation! I know you didn't like what she said about me at Bible study but she has to treat me like that! She has to talk about me hard like that! I'm so hard that I need that. You don't understand. She has to do it! I DESERVE IT! I know you are thinking about leaving. If you leave, it's going to give people the wrong idea about my bishop. You will tell people what happened and it will make the church look bad. All of this is my fault! You just don't understand how I am! It's me! I don't know why I do it! She has to treat me like this! She has to talk to me like this!"

Pseuda is very intelligent. She repeated many of the messages that she heard the bishop teach in Bible study verbatim. When she stopped to catch her breath, I gave her some very pointed comments. Knowing that she would repeat everything that I said, I told her what I wanted her to take back. She did not disappoint me. Although she arrived at my home at approximately 10:00 p.m.

supposedly to end her relationship with Joe, at 4:00 a.m., she was still there. She talked herself to sleep. She went to sleep with her head lying on Joe's shoulder and her arm stretched across him.

At 8:00 a.m., I received a phone call from Pseuda. She wanted me and Joe to meet with her and the bishop. The reason for this meeting escaped me. By 4:00 a.m., I thought everything had been resolved. That was when I woke her up and she left. With Pseuda's continuous insistence, I reluctantly agreed to the meeting.

The meeting was held at 9:00 p.m. at the church. For some reason that was unknown to me, Minister Jack and Elder Minni were also included in the meeting. Although they had no direct involvement in what was being discussed, they remained throughout the session. They were also permitted to provide input and ask questions. The session began and ended without prayer. It lasted for over two hours. There were two other women at the church during this time. They were in an adjoining office. One of them was Airel, who was interested in Joe. Needless to say, they listened to the complete drama.

It began with Pseuda repeating her conversation of the previous evening. I also repeated the comments that I had given

Pseuda to take back. During the time that Joe was being enlightened about all the reasons that he should not become involved with Pseuda, she was told repeatedly that she was not his type and that he was using her. Since some of the people that had been feeding both of them were sitting at the table, Joe assured them that he was still interested in her despite everything that had been said about her.

As the meeting went on, it became increasingly dramatic. Saturday Night Live is unable to compete with what happened in that room. There were at least two actors at the table. They both deserve an Oscar or some award close to it. My writing skills lack the ability to communicate the calamity of the situation.

Eventually, I conveyed that Pseuda had been at my home until 4:00 a.m. At this point, everything shifted. It was finally understood why we were unmoved or concerned about how passionate Pseuda's declarations were.

Bishop Aines banged her hand on the table and exclaimed, "OH! Oh! I understand why he's not upset by what you are saying; he knows you don't mean it. It took you how long to break it off?"

Pseuda chimed in, "What?! What?! We didn't have sex!"

Bishop Aines screamed at her, "It's worse than that! You were touching and agreeing! You were touching and agreeing!"

Pseudo repeated herself, "What?! What?! We didn't have sex! It's not like we had sex or anything!"

Bishop Aines retorted back at her, "Don't you know when two or more touch and agree God is in the midst! No wonder Dr. Charlotte was wondering what we were meeting about. You left her house at 4:00 a.m. and called me at 7:30 a.m. It was 9:00 p.m. when you told me you were going to break up with him. I thought you were going to the restaurant to meet him. You didn't tell me you were going to the house!"

By this time, I was no longer able to hold back my laughter. Everyone else in the room was laughing, except Pseuda and Joe. Pseuda was quiet. Joe was shaking his head.

Bishop Aines turned to me and asked, "Dr. Charlotte, did you think I didn't want them to see each other?"

To this question, I responded, "Yes!"

Bishop Aines clearly stated, "I didn't have anything to do with it! I don't have a problem with them dating. As long as they're dating in a healthy relationship, they don't have to be creeping and sneaking around with each other. If she wants to be with him, they should just date openly in a healthy way. If this is what they really want, then she needs to leave me out of it. She called me early this morning. I should have stayed at home with my husband! He tried to tell me not fool with this mess! I can't believe this! I'm not trying to keep them apart!"

Before the meeting ended, Elder Minni made the reason known for her presence. Pseuda had informed Bishop Aines of my concerns about the meeting between Joe and Elder Minni. Those differences had already been resolved. During a brief dialogue, Elder Minni again called Airel a *hoe*. She also reiterated her previous comments about Airel.

Minister Jack's reason for being there is unclear. It may have been related to his continued involvement in everything that had taken place. Throughout the meeting, he stressed how close he was to Pseuda. On many occasions, he told me he found her disgusting. Minister Jack rarely speaks kindly of any woman.

The meeting was abruptly ended; I believed that everything had been resolved and the secrecy would stop. As we prepared to exit the building, Airel, walked down the hall with Elder Minni. Airel resides with her. After hearing what was said about her, Airel was hysterical. When we exited the building, Bishop Aines was trying to calm her.

For a couple of days, Pseuda was pleasant towards me at church. She was always friendly during her regular trips to my house. She was also openly conversing with Joe at church. This didn't last through the week. She returned to her odd behavior.

He has removed our sins as far from us as the east is from the west.
Psalm 103:12 NLT

East and west can never meet. This expression is a symbolic portrait of God's forgiveness. When God forgives our sin, He separates it from us and He never remembers it. God forgives and forgets. We tend to dredge up or dwell on the ugliness of our past but God has wiped the record clean. When we follow God, we model His forgiveness. When we forgive, we must also forget the pain of the wound. Otherwise, we have not truly forgiven that person.

Things continued to spin out of control. On more than one occasion, I thought the issue was settled. Later, secrecy and blame would return. Pseuda and Joe seldom spoke at church. Whenever she came to our house, she used the back roads.

On November 6, 2011, Pseuda picked Joe up from a local restaurant, as we were having lunch with a group from the church. Although she was treated cordially by those in the group, she displayed warmth for only one person, Joe.

When Joe returned home, he told me what had happened while he was with Pseuda. Joe stated that Bishop had called her. He was sitting next to Pseuda throughout their conversation. She was calling concerning Pseuda's relationship with him.

After the preliminaries, Bishop Aines asked, "Do you plan to continue seeing Joe?"

Pseuda responded, "Yes! But we won't be sleeping together nor having sex."

Bishop Aines responded, "I can't believe you still want to talk to him after everything that you have lost!"

Pseuda took a deep breath but did not respond.

The bishop continued, "The devil has used him to destroy your ministry, your relationship with your pastor, your reputation, and your integrity. You're telling me that you still want to stay attached to him?"

Pseuda responded, "Yes! I still want to be attached to him but not the sin."

Even after this, the conversation continued for an extended period of time. During the conversation, Bishop Aines told Pseuda, "If you are going to continue seeing him, the relationship needs to be moving towards engagement."

After learning the drama was ongoing, I wanted to discover the complete truth. By this time, I was convinced that there was more than one deceiver. In this effort to bring things out in the open and stop the confusion, I contacted Bishop Aines via facebook.com email. I wanted everything in writing so there would be no more wavering. The emails follow.

November 7, 2011
Charlotte Russell Johnson:
Good morning Bishop,
I am seriously worried about Pseuda's relationship with Joe. She has never stopped seeing him. She called him the night after we had the meeting and she is on the phone with him 6-8 hours every day. She still is acting rude towards me but it has increased. I have told Joe that if they continue their relationship in secret, people will assume that they have something to hide. For whatever reason, she still wants to play this game. Yes, she is a manipulator. However, I am concerned that there is a much deeper problem. He doesn't need this drama in his life and I am certainly tired of it. What can we do to stop it? I am praying hard. I like Pseuda and she has a lot of potential. If she does not change her pattern of behavior, she will BE detrimental to his ministry. My prayers for their relationship have changed. I'm praying, "If she is not the woman for him that GOD will drive a wedge between them to separate them as far as the east is from the west."

HAVE A BLESSED DAY!

November 7, 2011
Bishop Aines:
Good morning Dr. C.,
I know exactly what you are saying....Just last
night I went to her again and asked her why is she
doing this? She had no answer to give. I talked for
about an hour and for the most part she just
listened without saying too much of anything. I
really think she doesn't want to have anything to
do with you because she don't want you to know
what is really going on. I feel this is an attack of
the enemy and I have done all I can do to stay one
step ahead. She has never acted this bad even
though she has done some crazy stuff before. I
asked her last night that if she really want to be
"friends" with Joe, why don't she be "friends"
with him in a healthy, non sexual relationship in
the open instead of in secrecy. She said because
she don't want to be with him like that! Of
course...I went in on her but needless to say...she
blocked me out! I certainly don't want her to be
detrimental to his ministry and I feel that the
enemy is using her in some way to destroy him.
She does what she wants with him and then puts
him on blast by telling some vulgar stuff against
him. I ask her well if he's this or that...why do you
want him? AND again her answer was "I don't
know". I touch and agree with you for the prayer
and let's watch God change things! Oh and just so
you will know....I am going to constantly stay in
her face about this...until the enemy gets tired and
flee!
Blessings to you!

November 7, 2011
Charlotte Russell Johnson:
It's all game. She tells him everything.
She is acting as if you are trying to separate them.
I am really concerned about her mental health.

November 7, 2011
Bishop Aines:
Yes I know.....I just finish talking with her again.
She said that the reason she treats you this way is
because she was hoping you will pull Joe away
from her and she won't have to deal with him. She
also stated that Joe calls her more then she calls
him and that after last night she told him not to
call her and that he's been trying but she refuses to
answer. She told me that she is done! I told her
that she was hurting his ministry and she agreed!
Of course, we both know how that goes. She said
she only uses him to make her feel loved! He feels
a void by telling her he loves her. I told her that
she had low self esteem. And you are absolutely
right...it is a mental thing. I told her she was
drawing up a fairy tale relationship in her head
and trying to live it out. She as foolish as it
sounds...admitted to all of her nasty, manipulating,
controlling ways that we talked on. She also
admitted that this is a game!

November 7, 2011
Charlotte Russell Johnson:
Lies again. He was with her when you called her
yesterday. She is not dating him secretly. She is
hiding it from you. She is taking this crazy talk
both ways and she is blaming you for them not
being able to be open. He goes to sleep at night

with her on the phone. She talks so much she doesn't know he is sleep.

There was no response after this email. Later that night, I stopped by the church. The pastor asked me to come inside. She stated that Pseuda was constantly saying vile things about Joe. She further stated that there were three people who could verify this information. She asked Elder Minni, Minister Jack, and her personal assistant to accompany us into a classroom. Neither of them was able to provide any vile information.

We were aware of vile information that Pseuda spread about Joe. In an effort to eliminate Airel, whom she viewed as competition, Pseuda became overly friendly with her. She then pretended to do a personality assessment on Joe. She did not bother to consult him for the information that would be needed. She never did a psychological assessment or evaluation on him. Although she is not qualified to administer these tests, Pseuda has taken classes in college related to this field. She proceeded to give Joe a DSM-IV mental health diagnosis. Pseuda then shared the false assessment with him and Airel. It was believable to Airel. Pseuda told Airel that she was wise not to pursue a relationship with Joe. As she was doing all this, Pseuda was actively pursuing her relationship with Joe.

When I learned that Pseuda was deceiving Airel, I warned Joe that Airel was going to be hurt when she discovered the truth. Within hours, Airel overheard him talking to Pseuda on the telephone. She was extremely upset. Although I was not at the church and had nothing to do with the deception, Airel began a verbal assault against me. Joe retaliated by saying something equally as hurtful to Airel. Information about her past history had been shared with him by several members of the church. Bishop Aines had to intervene to settle the dispute. This happened several weeks before the current meeting with the bishop and her assistants.

After the assistants failed to provide the vile information, Bishop Aines continued her defense. Nothing could have prepared me for what happened at that time. I have seen people play many games inside and outside of the church. When it comes to cell phones, the games seem limitless. Those who play these games seldom allow others to witness the games. Let me be clear, I have never seen another

pastor play this one.

In the presence of four witnesses, the bishop called Pseuda and placed the phone on speaker phone. She asked everyone in the room to remain quiet. Pseuda was never told that others were in the room. Why it was necessary for them to hear this conversation is a mystery to me. Most pastors understand that communications made to them by a person seeking spiritual help or guidance is confidential and privileged.

Confidentiality places an obligation on ministers if not a legal responsibility. Clergy malpractice is defined as a breach of the duty by a member of the clergy (e.g., trust, loyalty, confidentiality, guidance) that results in harm or loss to a church member. Usually, a claim for clergy malpractice asserts that a minister should be held liable for professional misconduct or an unreasonable lack of competence in their capacity as a religious leader and counselor.

Most clergy malpractice cases are couched in terms of Tort Law as matters of alleged negligence, abuse of authority or power, inappropriate conduct, breach of confidentiality and trust, or incompetence. The claims assert that ministers owe the same kind of duty to persons they serve as doctors, counselors, or lawyers owe to clients.

Therefore doth Job open his mouth in vain; he
multiplieth words without knowledge.
Job 35:16

Pseuda was never advised of her
Miranda rights. It was not a court of law but
every wrong word would be used against
her. She was never told that others were
listening to their conversation. Throughout
her conversation with Pseuda, the pastor
attempted to guide the conversation.

The young woman seemed to be
suspicious and repeatedly asked, "Why are
you taking me through all this?! Are you
trying to prove something to someone?! Is
someone listening to our conversation?!"

Let no man deceive you with vain words: for
because of these things cometh the wrath of
God upon the children of disobedience.
Ephesians 5:5-7

Deceptively, Bishop Aines replied, "I'm
trying to make sure I understand what you
said!"

Pseuda was not convinced and replied,
"Why?! Why?! I did everything that you said.
I talked to him real hard today! I did it just
like you told me; why are you taking me
through this?!"

The more Bishop Aines tried to steer
the conversation, the more convinced I was

that she was the center of the confusion. Pseuda repeated many conversations that she had shared with the bishop concerning Joe. Each time that Pseuda contradicted the bishop's declaration of innocence, she attempted to cut her off.

At one point, Pseuda said with irritation in her voice, "I don't know why we have to go through all this! When we had the last meeting, you said that we could date!"

Evidently forgetting I was there or assuming I was simple minded, Bishop Aines replied, "If I told you to go to hell, would you go!?"

After being unsuccessful in leading Pseuda in the desired direction, Bishop Aines ended the call. The whole thing left me wondering who was crazy. After hearing the conversation, her assistants continued to insist that Bishop Aines had nothing to do with what was happening. As I have often heard, "I was born one night but it wasn't last night." Later, I learned what Pseuda meant by talking hard to Joe; her words were laced with extreme profanity.

After this conversation, I said very little. My concern about this ministry was peeking. This was not a place that I could continue to recommend. There are many people who respect my opinion. Joe had grown to love the ministry. He was not deceived by the things going on there. It is my belief that he hated to leave Pseuda there. Certainly, I hated to leave Joe there.

The next week another incident happened, it caused me grave concern. During a leadership meeting, the pastor made this angry declaration, "IF anyone comes back to the altar for deliverance and they are not ready, I am going to pray a curse on them that it is going to take God to remove." This was witchcraft! My mind was made up! With or without Joe, I was leaving!

Bishop Aines is enamored with the Old Testament and the curses found in this portion of the scriptures. She rarely teaches from the New Testament accept the book of Revelations. The doctrine of grace and mercy are severely lacking in her teaching. When she threatened to curse God's people, she sincerely believed she had the power and authority to do so.

Finally, I confessed all my sins to You and stopped trying to hide my guilt. I said to myself, "I will confess my rebellion to the LORD." And you forgave me! All my guilt is gone.
Psalm 32:5 NLT

To confess our sin is to agree with God's opinion about the act or situation. Although we may feel overwhelmed by the multitude and magnitude of our sins, God will forgive them all. If we ask Him sincerely, He will restore us to right standing with Him. No one is beyond redemption. No one is so full of sin that they can't be made clean. The atoning blood of Jesus Christ is sufficient enough to atone for all our sins. The blood is able to heal the very wound of sin. God is not willing that any should perish. He wants all of us to come to Him in repentance. He is able to keep all that are committed to Him. No man can curse what God has blessed and no man bless what God has cursed.

For the LORD God is our sun and our shield. He gives us grace and glory. The LORD will withhold no good thing from those who do what is right.

Psalm 84:11 NLT

God will not hold anything back that will help us in serving Him. If He chooses to withhold anything from us, it is because it's harmful to His purpose in our life. Don't let anyone deceive you with vain words or empty philosophies. Put your trust in God. When you fall, never stop repenting. Ask God to deliver you and you will no longer fall. Touching the hem of His garment will provide oil for your wounds.

The Letter

and you have forgotten the exhortation which is addressed to you as sons, "Joe, do not regard lightly the discipline of the Lord, nor faint when you are reproved by Him.
Hebrews 12:5 NAS

When I came to this ministry, my only desire was to aid with the social programs that the church was reportedly planning to launch. Within two weeks, I became painfully aware that God had another purpose for me. It is my honest belief that God sent me to warn them about their deceptive practices and allow them space to repent before God sends judgment. God's purpose was fulfilled the day that I left there.

Truthful lips will be established forever but a lying tongue is only for a moment.
Proverbs 12:19 NAS

This church has regular leadership meetings. During these meetings, it is common to discuss other pastors, ministries, and those who have left the church. It was during these encounters that it was discussed that a local pastor had called this group a cult. The pastor that this assertion was attributed to is highly respected and I value his opinion. It is not an opinion that I would dismiss lightly. My spiritual senses were on alert. While I continued to be faithful, I was watching and praying. Joe was also watching and praying. He was also hoping things would change.

I love the LORD because he hears my voice and my prayer for mercy. Because he bends down to listen, I will pray as long as I have breath!
Psalm 116:1-2, NLT

God is so responsive to the prayers of His children that you can always reach Him. He bends down and listens to your voice. This writer's love for the Lord had grown because he had experienced answers to His prayers. If you are discouraged, remember that God is near. He is listening carefully to each and every prayer. He is answering each prayer in order to give His children, His best.

This church is obsessed with demonic activities. It is not uncommon to refer to those who leave the ministry as being demon possessed. Knowing these things about the ministry and because of my personal observation of their handling of business matters, I chose to tender my resignation in writing and in great detail. To avoid error, I gave those who would be in attendance at my tribunal a copy of this notice.

It was my desire that the information

shared with the leadership of that organization would serve as the tool to aid them in becoming a church that would bring glory and honor to God. It was never my intention that it would be made public. After an open attack was made against me on facebook.com, this was no longer an option.

Prior to my written notice, there were several meetings and conversations with this pastor. All of these were held in a very unprofessional manner. Members were discussed who were not in attendance. Intimate details about their past, their families, and sexual history were often shared in open conversation. Members were present who had no direct bearing on the situation. It was reported on facebook.com that I left this ministry for reasons that are inconsistent with my true reason for leaving; a portion of this letter is included below. Only my most serious concerns are shared.

November 11, 2011
To the Pastor, Deacons, and Elders
These actions were not taken lightly but after much thought and prayer. I decided to state these reasons for my leaving in writing for the sake of clarity and accuracy, rather than contributing to the rumors that have been circulating for some time. Also, please know that there is no hidden agenda or purpose.

Simply put, my reason for resigning from

Thespian Church is a loss of confidence in the leadership ...With the leading of the Lord and submission to His will and authority, these things can be easily corrected. Indeed they should be corrected immediately in order to enable this ministry to bring glory and honor to His name.

Several months ago, we were delighted to attend and join Thespian Church ...we considered ourselves blessed to have found a good church. In saying we, I am including Joe. We have made many friends at Thespian Church, and we hope you continue to be our friends after learning the reasons for my taking the steps that I now taking.

This request is being made after many months of soul searching and studying on my part. ...are not leaving because of hurt feelings, or being offended by anyone in the church. I have had to base my decision on my faith in the Lord and Savior Jesus Christ, my biblical education, my secular education, and my intellect. Every effort was made to be fair to you in this analytical assessment. It was only after meeting with you twice and hearing both conflicting and confusing messages that this decision is being made.

Please understand that I am taking this action because it has been proven to me that many of the teachings are false, and this ministry does not teach correct doctrine according to the gospel of Jesus Christ. After hearing repeatedly that Thespian Church is a cult, I began to investigate the characteristics of a cult and to carefully observe the behavior of church members. After careful evaluation, it has been determined that Thespian

Church meets all of the qualifications. Some of the doctrinal problems we have investigated are:

1. The group is focused on a living leader to whom members seem to display excessively zealous, unquestioning commitment. Members have openly stated that the pastor saved their souls or lives. This is a distinction that belongs to God.

2. The group is preoccupied with bringing in new members.

3. The group is preoccupied with making money.

4. Questioning, doubt, and dissent are discouraged or even punished. This includes emotional abuse or manipulation. Religious leaders should treat congregants with dignity, respect, and compassion and lead their congregations with humility and integrity, remaining aware of their influence over congregants and of their personal struggles. You have referred to members as hoes (whores) and faggots repeatedly.

5. Mind-numbing techniques (such as meditation, chanting, speaking in tongues, denunciation sessions, and debilitating work routines) are used to suppress doubts about the group and its leader(s).

6. The leadership dictates sometimes in great detail how members should think, act, and feel (for example members must get permission from leaders to date, change jobs, get married; leaders may prescribe what types of clothes to wear, where to live, how to discipline children, and so forth). Members are consistently told that they are too soft in disciplining their bad children. Examples include punching children under seven in their shoulder, slapping their heads, and giving them more than 25

licks. The Bible tells us not to spare the rod but it also tells us not to provoke our children to wrath. After two children were beaten excessively, they were told, "You want some more of me? Is that what you want? You don't want me!" The treatment of some children is not only tantamount to child abuse, it is neglect.

7. The group is elitist, claiming a special, exalted status for itself, its leader(s), and members (for example: the leader is considered the Messiah or an avatar; the group and/or the leader have a special mission to save humanity).

8. The group has a polarized us-versus-them mentality, which causes conflict with the wider society. You stated, "If you have had sex with someone outside of marriage and you continue in a relationship with that person, you are attaching yourself to the sin. Even if you are not having sex, you are still attaching yourself to the sin. They are not going to marry you. You are out of order. To continue even without the sex, it's the same as a crack addict returning to a crack house!" In your analogy, you forgot the story of David and Bathsheba. They suffered the consequences of their sin but were not required to divorce. Under your proclamation, this would also serve to say that most married couples are attached to sin because they had sex with their spouse prior to marriage.

9. The group's leader is not accountable to any authorities (as... military commanders and ministers, of mainstream denominations). You stated, "There is no one that you can tell on me!"

10. The group teaches or implies that its supposedly

exalted ends justify means that members would have considered unethical before joining the group (for example: collecting money for bogus charities). Members are openly discussed in the presence of other members. Confidentiality is nonexistent. Professional relationships commonly bound by such standards are those between a client and her lawyer, financial institution, or religious leader. Sharing confidential information is often a professional violation and a legal violation. There are a wide range of consequences that can result, including the payment of financial damages. Allowing or encouraging members to listen to telephone conversations with other members where the member is unaware that they are on speaker phone is a violation of confidentiality.

11. The leadership induces guilt feelings in members in order to control them. Claiming that someone is going to hell for disobeying the leader. Threatening to place a curse upon members, as you did on Monday, November 7, 2011. You threatened, "IF anyone comes back to the altar for deliverance and they are not ready, I am going to pray a curse on them that it is going to take God to remove."

12. Members' subservience to the group causes them to cut ties with family and friends, and to give up personal goals and activities that were of interest before joining the group.

13. Members are expected to devote inordinate amounts of time to the group.

14. Members are encouraged or required to live and/or socialize only with other group members.
On November 11, 2011, you took things to a

different level in usurping the authority of God. On facebook.com, you posted, "Shut the government down! Close the banks! Close the schools! For unto us a Child is born, Unto us a daughter is given; And the government will be upon her shoulders!"...

In closing, I wish to tell you my greatest reason for leaving Thespian Church. I do not want to be associated with an oppressive religion that dictates every aspect of the members lives. I know that my name is associated with good, moral character and teachings outside of Thespian Church, and I will continue to teach integrity and the most important of Christ's teachings: The love of their fellowman. This love is not isolated or elitist. It does not belittle the members, curse them, threaten them, call them degrading and derogatory names, or threaten to cause them bodily harm.

I realize that in your own opinion the decision I have made is a drastic one that entails eternal consequences. I ... look forward to the eternal consequences. I have accepted God's free gift of eternal life (Rom. 6:23). This is not only immortality ...

I hope that this letter has not seemed unfriendly, for I certainly have no personal malice toward you or any member of your church.

I will thank the LORD because He is just; I will sing praise to the name of the LORD Most High. Psalm 7:17, NLT

During a time of great evil and injustice, David was grateful that God is always righteous. When we wonder if anyone is honest or fair, we can be assured that God will continue to bring justice and fairness when we involve Him in our activities. In the midst of this, He also brings what we do not deserve, grace. If you ever feel that you are being treated unfairly, ask the one who is always fair and just to be with you. He is a just judge. Then give thanks to Him for His presence.

When I decide to leave the ministry, Joe had not fully decided when he would leave. My resignation was tendered on a Sunday after church. Leadership meeting was the following night. Joe went to the meeting. His purpose in going was to observe and discern. As the meeting was ending, some people were asked to leave the room. A second meeting was held. As the walls inside of this church are thin, Joe went to an adjoining room. He was able to hear everything that was said.

Yet they succeed in everything they do. They do not see your punishment awaiting them. They sneer at all their enemies.
Psalm 10:5 NLT

As she had done with many those who previously left the ministry, Bishop Aines accused me of having a spirit of witchcraft. She further stated that I wanted to destroy *her* ministry. She questioned several people in the room. Some were badgered. Pseuda did what she does best, whatever Bishop Aines says. Nothing that was done surprised me. It happened as I expected. One positive thing came from this meeting; Joe was convinced he needed to leave this church.

For a period, Joe's pain was severe. He had great admiration for this pastor. He was involved in the church. He had many friends there. He enjoys socializing. Many of them were going to turn against him. He was going to be treated as an outcast. Socialization was not a valid reason to stay there.

In standing for righteousness, there are penalties to pay. In deciding to leave this church, we weighed the options. Stay and support foolishness; those who support it will accept you. Go with the status quo; those who practice this foolishness will accept you. Stand up for God; God will always support you. If you lose anything for God and He will reward you. There was only one choice.

The devil wanted to use the deception at this church to destroy Joe. It was an attempt to get him to turn away from God. It was praying time. It was time for intense prayer. God is faithful! It didn't take long for the pain to begin to subside. For this wound, God had the oil. He generously poured it on our wounds.

Sin and Slander

Before I was afflicted I went astray but now I keep Your word. You are good and do good; Teach me Your statutes. The arrogant have forged a lie against me; With all my heart I will observe Your precepts. Their heart is covered with fat but I delight in Your law. It is good for me that I was afflicted, That I may learn Your statutes.
Psalm 119:67-71 NAS

When negative things happen in our lives, it can cause us to become discouraged or disheartened. Bitterness can easily creep in. When these things happen inside the church, it becomes easier for people to get severely wounded.

Because of the multitude of things that happened in my life, I have determined not to let bitterness, hatred, and unforgiveness reign. Over the years, I have been hurt numerous times in the church. In the process of writing this book, I was hurt multiple times. Disappointment with some people that I consider God's representatives also caused wounds.

Because in many cases, the church has strayed so far away from godly principles, I was tempted to walk away from an organized church. However, I was never tempted to walk away from God. Faithful friends were interceding for us. Strangers offered words of encouragement and prayer. Many true Christians were not afraid to stand up for righteousness. There were some who were more concerned about being politically or religiously correct. The concern for status exceeds the concern for righteousness.

There are numerous churches popping up each year. Rather than making access to holiness more available, in many cases they have clouded the view. The lure of the mega-churches and tele-evangelist has caused many to start their own churches while being ill-equipped for the task. Rather than following biblical guidelines or seeking seminary education, they follow the lead of prominent preachers.

This is not to say that television and radio have only negatively influenced the cause of Christ. Indeed, they have aided the spread of the gospel. Yet, where good is present, evil is always present. Where there are positives, there are also negatives. We have to be careful. Jesus is the plumb line.

A good name is rather to be chosen than great riches, and loving favour rather than silver and gold.
Proverbs 22:1

Billy Graham is the most prominent preacher of the last century. He has preached the gospel in person to more people than any other person in recorded history. According to his staff, more than 3.2 million people have responded to the invitation to salvation at his crusades around the world. At one revival in Seoul, South Korea, Reverend Graham attracted more than one million people to a single service. He has preached to live audiences of nearly 215 million people in more than 185 countries. He has also reached hundreds of millions more through television, video, film, and webcasts. As of 2008, Graham's lifetime audience, including radio and television broadcasts, reportedly exceeded 2.2 billion.

Whether this is true or not, I cannot tell. However, I heard this story about him. In the early days of his ministry, after giving the altar call, no one responded. It is said that he returned to his hotel room and cried. When a friend found him in tears, he asked what was wrong. Reverend Graham reportedly replied, "No one responded to the altar call." His friend responded, "Don't you know why?" Reverend Graham responded, "No! Why?" The friend answers, "You failed to lift up Jesus!" It said that the evangelist never made this mistake again. Even if this story is untrue, the moral of the story is profound.

Reverend Graham has consistently

ranked among the most admired persons in the United States and the world. Despite all of this, there has been no hint of scandal associated with his personal life or ministry. By all accounts, he is considered a man of integrity and the highest Christian and moral standards.

Howbeit that this is not the example that most Christians choose to follow. Billy Graham lacks the flair and glamor that many Christians ascribe to. He preaches a very simple message of the cross. Which evangelist in the last one hundred years can touch his record or example?

"Behold, I send you forth as sheep in the midst of wolves: be ye therefore wise as serpents, and harmless as doves. But beware of men: for they will deliver you to the councils, and they will scourge you in their synagogues; And ye shall be brought before governors and kings for my sake, for a testimony against them and the Gentiles" Matthew 10:16-18

Below is a letter that was posted on facebook.com concerning me and Joe. I will not address the claims in this letter individually. This was written after I gave written notification that I was leaving the church. It was also after I reposted an article about cults on my facebook.com page. It was an article that clearly identified the author. I was not that author. While reading the post, many people attached to that church identified with the article. Due to the information in the article, they rushed to judgment. They assumed the article was about them. The post below appeared on facebook.com. It was written by Pseuda, the young lady who was discussed in the emails that were shared in the previous chapter.

Sin and Slander
by Pseuda on Wednesday, November 16, 2011 at 12:06pm

Dr. Charlotte Russell Johnson, author of A Journey to Hell and Back and several other books came to Thespian Outreach ministries to support her son Joe. I later became involved with her son and this soon after became a very sinful relationship. Dr. Charlotte was in support of this relationship even though she knew that it was not a healthy one. My bishop intervened and told me to consider my actions after I had come to her to tell her what had been going on. Dr. Charlotte had told me on various occasions including a meeting with her, my bishop, and other ministers and elders that I was the reason that she had come to the church and she had also said that I would never be rid of her. She had even said on one occasion that I was supposed to be her Ruth and she my Naomi but I told her that my bishop was my Naomi and she said "well you go marry her son then." These remarks clearly led me to believe that she was not interested in my spiritual welfare but in being connected to me by way of her son. Throughout this back and forth (waivering) that I perpetuated she felt as if the church was what was keeping me from her grasp and as long as I was still being cordial and talking to her and her son she had no objections and insisted that every time I had left the sinful relationship that I would be back making comments like "Oh she want Joe", and "She'll be back". She stayed at the ministry working on the altar ministry, leading prayer over the house, participating in worship services, and working with the perfecting the saints class which she was a part of the development of Christian education. She did all of these things faithfully until I would no longer allow her to be a part of my life or be cordial with her. I had completely cut her off and then she called a meeting with the bishop saying that her prayers now had changed and that I was being rude to her and she didn't understand why so she now prays that me and her son be separated as far as the east is from the west and that I was damaging to his ministry. I then decided that I would no longer live in this sinful lifestyle anymore and cut off her son, I said that this was completely my decision and that I am to blame for any confusion that either of them may have had and that my own desires are what led to this. They insisted that it was my church and My bishop that had too much control over my life, and I told them that My bishop was only intervening to make me aware of the consequences of my decisions and actions just as any true spiritual leader should do to a member of their flock, attempting to save my soul from the fiery furnace toward which I was headed. She at no time forbid me to do anything and always made me aware that my decisions are my own and that God is who I have to answer to. Since this time Dr. Charlotte has given out slanderous propaganda to various members of the ministry, calling this ministry a cult and making several untrue allegations regarding the woman of God and the ministry as a whole. She is bashing the ministry and the leader in a very demonic way. She possesses the spirit of witchcraft and has spoken very badly of many other churches in the area. All ministries please BEWARE!!!! A follow up letter will be sent to all leaders in the area.

End the evil of those who are wicked, and defend the righteous. For You look deep within the mind and heart, O righteous God.
Psalm 7:9 NLT

Nothing is ever hidden from God's view. This can be either very terrifying or extremely comforting. Our thoughts are an open book to Him. Because He knows even our motives, we have no place to hide. There is no way to pretend that we can get away with sin. But that very knowledge also gives us great comfort. We don't have to impress God or put up a false shield. Instead, we can trust God to help us work through all our weaknesses. This will enable us to serve Him as He has planned. When we truly follow God, He rewards our effort.

"But for the cowardly and unbelieving and abominable and murderers and immoral persons and sorcerers and idolaters and all liars, their part will be in the lake that burns with fire and brimstone, which is the second death."
Revelation 21:8 NAS

Within moments of the previous post posting to facebook.com, this posted:

Bishop Aines:
Can you believe this? A minister and her son wanted to fornicate with others in my ministry and when they were asked to leave the mother decided to bad mouth and question my leadership as she did other churches that she was associated with. Angry with me she proceeded to write letters to say we are a cult. If living holy and righteous makes me a part of a cult then count me in. Lol. Case of slander!

Several people commented on the above post. They assumed that the information was true. If they had compared the post from Pseuda with this one, the deception would have been obvious. There were a few godly people who showed wisdom in their responses. Although I do not know the bishop that posted this comment, he attempted to bring wisdom in this situation.

Bishop B: Jesus did not condemn the woman

caught in the act of adultry YES they are wrong and they are to be punished and rebukeed openly but we as leaders must posess the love of Jesus christ so we can save the lost and dying people in the church that are on their way to hell

This is the response that he received.

Bishop Aines @ Bishop B, sir I did all I could do to make this right. After several meetings with this woman and her son and those involved that wanted this harassment to stop she would get more and more angry with me and tell me that sexual immorality is not a sin. Never did I rebuke her openly this was done in private. She became even more unruly and started to slander the leadership of my husband and I to the partakers of the ministry. My mission is and always will be the lost.

The bishop's husband has never taught anything that was deviation from sound biblical truths in my presence. He has carried himself in a manner that reflects godly principles. He was never present when these meetings occurred. He has never said anything derogatory about any member of the church to me or Joe. Indeed, we both continue to respect him and his walk with God.

As far as my position on sin, I struggle with legalism. Anyone who knows me personally is aware of this fact. I do not condone secular music being played in the church. It bothered me when alcohol was brought into the church for an alternative to Halloween celebration. Church members dancing in a provocative manner during that event also disturbed me. I even have issues with non-alcoholic wine being served at Christian events. This can serve as a trigger for a recovering alcoholic. My opinions are so strong that at times I dare not share them. My beliefs about sin have been shared in each of my books.

> Minister Jack: a cult but just last week she was reading the prayer over the congregation...smh I'm the one who passed her a mic LOL if we are a cult than what is she??? Sounds like mamma was trying to hook her son up and it didn't work! The things people do Smh!

LORD, have mercy on me. See how my enemies torment me. Snatch me back from the jaws of death. Save me so I can praise You publicly at Jerusalem's gates, so I can rejoice that You have rescued me.
Psalm 9:13-14 NLT

Some very wise people requested that this information be removed from facebook.com. It was removed but not before the damage was done. Strangers contacted me about the information. At the time, I was advised not to comment. Now that time has passed and the facts speak for themselves. The facts don't lie.

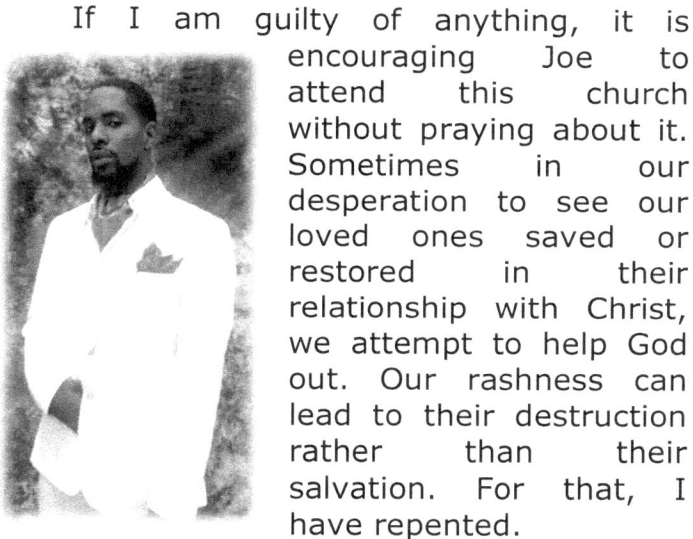

If I am guilty of anything, it is encouraging Joe to attend this church without praying about it. Sometimes in our desperation to see our loved ones saved or restored in their relationship with Christ, we attempt to help God out. Our rashness can lead to their destruction rather than their salvation. For that, I have repented.

All of us want God to help us when in trouble. However, our reasons for seeking His help are often for different reasons. Some want God's help so that they will be successful. They equate success with popularity. They believe if they are successful, other people will like them. Others want God's help so that they will be comfortable and self-assured. They want to feel good about themselves. David, however, wanted help from God so that justice would be restored to Israel.

Not to us, O LORD, not to us but to Your name goes all the glory for Your unfailing

love and faithfulness.
Psalm 115:1 NLT

This psalmist asked that God's name be glorified. All too often, we ask God to glorify His name with our plans. We may pray with selfish motives for help to do a good job. There is nothing wrong with having a spirit of excellence; the problem comes when we ignore God's reputation in the process. When praying, ask yourself, "Who will get the credit if God answers my prayer?"

When you call out to God for help, consider your motive. Is it to save you pain and embarrassment or to bring God glory and honor? If our purpose is to glorify God, He will pour oil into any wounds that we receive along the way. In this situation, I say, bring glory to Your name God.

Maintaining Integrity

People with integrity walk safely but those who
follow crooked paths will slip and fall.
Proverbs 10:9 NLT

Integrity is a high standard of living
based on a personal code of morality.
Integrity refuses to succumb to temporary
gratification or the dictates of the majority.
Integrity is to personal character what health
is to the body. Integrity is to personal
character what salvation is to the soul.
People who walk in integrity are upright.
Their lives are balanced. People with integrity
have nothing to hide and nothing to fear.
Their lives are an open book. They know that
the world is watching their behavior. They
are confident that under scrutiny, their
behavior will match their beliefs. They are
assured that their walk will match their talk.
They gladly assert that my character will
match my confession.

One morning upon our arrival at the
church, Minister Jack rushed from the
building to greet us. He seemed upset and
was waving his hand. Something was
obviously wrong.

He shouted, "Dr. Charlotte, come
directly into the building! Don't talk to the
people in that car!"

Prior to his instructions, the car had gone unnoticed by me. Not only was I unaccustomed to anyone telling me who not to speak to, my mother had instructed me from a child to speak to everyone. Mama always said, "The time of day belongs to anybody."

When Joe and I exited the car, we both spoke to the driver. While I didn't recognize her, she did recognize me.

After identifying herself, she asked, "Do you attend that Church?"

To this, I replied briefly, "Yes!"

She quickly followed up, "I need to talk to you about that church!"

As I had no idea what was happening, I responded, "OK!"

In spite of this, I continued to my destination inside the building. It would be easy to contact me at a later time. She has known my mother for several years. During that time, I have only heard positive things about her. In my presence, she has always carried herself in a professional Christian manner. Without knowing what was happening, I assumed that I would be able to aid in bringing about a peaceful resolution to the problem.

Minister Jack began to explain, "The police are on the way. She's trying to see Bishop Aines. Her daughter lives in a trailer that the church owns. We have been trying to get her to move out. She didn't honor the contract. We turned the lights out at the trailer to force her out. When we went by there the lights were back on. Her mother was there. We had a paper for the daughter but the mother took it out my hand. I snatched it back. She said that I hurt her arm. So now, she is over here wanting to see Bishop. We told her that she is not here but she won't leave. She better leave before I hit her for real. We called the police."

Wherefore putting away lying, speak every man truth with his neighbour: for we are members one of another.
Ephesians 4:25

Trying to sort it all out, I asked, "Where is Bishop Aines?"

Minister Jack responded, "She's on the phone!"

Raising the telephone receiver in her hand to enable me to see it, another minister responded, "She's in her office but she can't come out because we told the lady she wasn't here."

Somewhat shocked, I asked, "Does Bishop Aines know what's going on?"

The female minister responded, "She knows everything that is going on. She's been trying to get out of the back entrance of her office so she can walk up to the building as if she just got here. She can't get the door open."

Minister Jack inserted, "She better leave! I don't mind hitting a woman!"

At this point, I was at a real loss for words. Unsure how to respond, I just said nothing. The police arrived and after a few minutes, the woman left without further incident. At this point, Bishop Aines came out of the office. After explaining the situation to the officer, the officer advised them of the proper procedure to handle an eviction. When the officer left, I had finally gathered my thoughts.

Doesn't He see everything I do and every step I take? "Have I lied to anyone or deceived anyone? Let God weigh me on the scales of justice, for He knows my integrity.
Job 31:4-8 NLT

To Minister Jack, I said, "Regardless of the situation, you have to maintain your Christian integrity. There are ways to handle this type of situation. You didn't have a contract with the mother; there was no reason to get into a discussion or altercation with her..."

Before I could finish, Bishop Aines stopped me. Firmly, she said, "Un-uh! You don't have to let anybody handle you like that! You don't let them run over you!"

This shut my mouth. There was nothing left to say on that matter. However, I was thinking plenty of thoughts.

Integrity is not about reputation. It's not about what people think of us. Integrity is not about how successful we are. It's not even about what we have accomplished. Integrity embodies the sum total of our being and our actions.

Integrity originates in who we are as believers in Jesus Christ. As Christians, we are redeemed from the power of sin and death. We have been accepted into the family of God. We have value and worth because of God's grace. We are capable of living a holy and sanctified life because the Holy Spirit enables us to do so. All of this is expressed to the world by the way we live and behave. We are to maintain our integrity in every place and situation. We can't conveniently disregard it.

For the LORD gives wisdom; from His mouth come knowledge and understanding; He stores up sound wisdom for the upright; He is a shield to those who walk in integrity, guarding the paths of justice and watching over the way of His saints.
Proverbs 2:6-8

Unfortunately, integrity seems to be declining more and more each year. Often, our integrity is sacrificed for fame and fortune. Regretfully, what we desire to achieve is more important than what God has called us to be. Integrity is lost when we value expedience more than excellence. Integrity is sacrificed when personal progress becomes more important than holiness. When riches become more valuable than righteousness, integrity is lost.

People are watching our behavior. When we name the name of Christ, the scrutiny intensifies. They watch to see if our behavior matches our belief. They want to see if our walk matches our talk. They are watching to see if our character matches what we confess. In other words, the world is watching to see if we have integrity.

When people find that our integrity has not been compromised, they will value our relationship with Christ. When they have wounds that need healing, they will free to seek our help. They will trust us to pour oil into their wounds.

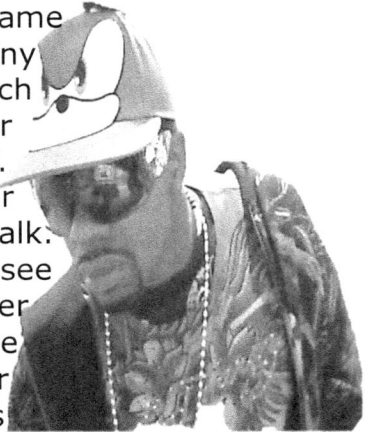

Use for the Useless

If your gift is to encourage others, be encouraging. If it is giving, give generously. If God has given you leadership ability, take the responsibility seriously. And if you have a gift for showing kindness to others, do it gladly.

Romans 12:8 NLT

If you believe people are consistently trying to use you, do an honest assessment. What is it that they want from you? Is it something they don't have access to? What do you have that God didn't give you? Is this same God capable of doing the same for them?

If you feel that you have nothing to offer, ask God to show you what He has placed in your hands. Ask Him to show you the gifts, talents, and abilities that He has uniquely given to you. Ask Him how you can use these things for His glory.

Good comes to those who lend money generously and conduct their business fairly.

Psalm 112:5 NLT

Generosity has the ability to cure two problems that money often creates. People often abuse others in their desire to accumulate wealth. Generosity will eliminate this tendency towards abuse. Moreover, the fear of losing money can be a snare. Generosity and respect for God places our trust in Him, not our money. God has the ability to provide justice, peace, happiness, and security.

We now have this light shining clay jars containing this great treasure. This makes it clear that our great power is from God, not from ourselves. We are pressed on every side by troubles but we are not crushed. We are perplexed but not in our hearts but we ourselves are like fragile driven to despair. We are hunted down but never abandoned by God. We get knocked down but we are not destroyed.
2 Corinthians 4:7-9 NLT

Every Christian is a vessel that God has uniquely created for sharing a treasure with others. This treasure, the gospel of Jesus, is contained in "fragile clay jars." Our great power is from God, not from ourselves. Paul uses the phrase "fragile clay jars" because as humans we are easily broken. We often struggle with the basic details of our life. In spite of this, we are called to pour out of our treasure into others. We are called to pour oil into the wounded. This is the way that God has ordained for the world to know Him.

God is awesome! Not long ago, I was having a Moses moment. I was feeling unqualified to complete the task that HE has assigned me. Despair had not fully surfaced but it was knocking on my door. Before it took control, my phone rang. A young lady was calling to give me a praise report!

Overjoyed, she said, "Do you remember me? It's been nine years since my release from jail. You came there and shared your testimony with us. I know sometimes it seems that we aren't listening but a lot of us get your message. I have been free of drugs and alcohol for nine years..."

As she continued, tears rolled down my checks. If we knew all our seeds that have taken root, we would become proud. But every now and then to encourage us to keep sowing, He gives us a glimpse of how He has used us. THANK YOU GOD for using Your unworthy servant.

These clay jars can eventually become empty from lack of use. Their substance evaporates. Empty vessels serve little purpose other than taking up valuable space. The Lord does not want us to merely exist. Each person has been made for a unique purpose. When a Christian is not connected

188

to the vine (the source of these gifts), their willingness and passion for serving God and other people diminishes.

Think about your life as a vessel today. How has it been used to store the goodness of God? Has the goodness leaked from the vessel to wasted places? Has that goodness flowed into the lives of others? Has God's measure of goodness in you evaporated from days and months of inactivity? Is your life like a vessel full of holes, leaking the goodness of God continuously? Is your vessel overflowing to others because you are continuously filled by the source that never runs dry? Is your vessel providing oil for the wounded?

For everything there is a season, a time for every activity under heaven.
Ecclesiastes 3:1

God is the source of all life. He makes everything perfect in its season. As Christians, we know that God causes everything to work together for the good of those who love God and are the called according to His purpose for them. Even the things that seem most painful in our lives have purpose. At times, the purpose is obscured by our tears.

The secret to peace with God is to determine, accept, and value God's perfect timing. We have to trust His timing and His plan. We have to keep turning back to Him. To doubt God's timing is to move ahead without His advice.

A recurrent theme throughout the book of Proverbs is, "All is vanity and vexation of spirit." The writer concludes that all things apart from God are empty and pointless. Solomon affirms the value of relationships, work, knowledge, and pleasure but only in their proper place. No joy, peace, happiness, or contentment is possible without God. We should strive to know God better and love Him more. He is the source of all wisdom, knowledge, peace, and joy. Every moment and every season is another opportunity to turn back to Him. It is another opportunity to make things right with Him. He is waiting for the opportunity to have a closer relationship with us.

> I lie awake thinking of You,
> meditating on You through the night.
> Psalm 63:6 NLT

During sleepless and uncomfortable nights, David thought about the goodness of God. Instead of counting sheep, he meditated on His Shepherd. He reviewed all the ways God had previously helped him. He greeted the next day with songs of praise and thanksgiving.

In quiet moments of loneliness or wakeful nights, use that time to count examples of God's faithfulness to you. Doing so is far more likely to give you rest than counting any other items that you might think of! This is another opportunity to renew our minds.

You have taught children and infants to
tell of Your strength, silencing Your enemies
and all who oppose You.
Psalm 8:2 NLT

Children are able to trust and praise God without doubts, hesitation, or reservations. As we grow older, many of us find this increasingly difficult to master. Ask God to give you childlike faith, removing any barriers and hindrances to having a closer walk with Him. Embrace the child inside of you. Get in touch with these childlike qualities inside of yourself so that you can be more openly expressive. Inside of you, there is oil for your wounds. God placed it there.

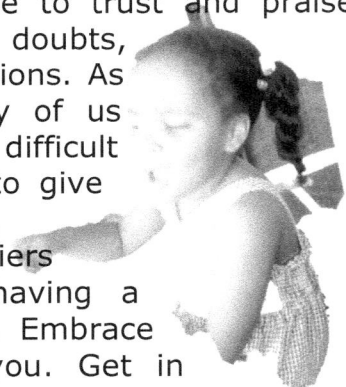

Self-Inflicted

And when his armourbearer saw that Saul was
dead, he fell likewise upon his sword,
and died with him.
1 Samuel 31:5

In recent weeks, the news has overwhelmed us with stories of suicides. Perhaps, the most shocking of all was that of Don Cornelius. He was a well-known cultural icon in the black community. The creator of "Soul Train" was found dead in his South Oaks, CA home from a gunshot wound to the head. Officials believe the wound was self-inflicted. "Soul Train" debuted in 1971 and ran until 2006. Although the icon found fame and fortune, there was something missing in the end. It is widely speculated that the declining health of the seventy-five-year-old entrepreneur led to his decision to end his life.

Many of the other suicides in the news were attributed to their impending criminal sentences. It appears, for some suicide was a more desirable outcome than a life behind prison bars. Some of these criminal charges were related to indecent behavior with children.

The death of a loved one is always painful. In the situations that have been mentioned, there is a measurable understanding of their actions. But what happens when a person who appears to be happy and balanced in life for no apparent decides to take their life? The family is left with additional pain. The unanswered questions are endless. Guilt and blame often run rampant. Those left to deal with the aftermath of a suicide often become wounded.

The experts say that opening up about suicide is crucial to the healing process. A loved one's suicide can trigger a wealth of emotions. These include but are not limited to shock, anger, guilt, blame, and despair. Other extreme reactions may continue during the weeks and months after a loved one's suicide. These include nightmares, flashbacks, loss of appetite, difficulty concentrating, social isolation, confusion, sleeplessness, and loss of interest in usual activities. These will be more intense if you witnessed or discovered the suicide.

If you are going through a grieving process, be careful to protect your own well-being. Be prepared for painful reminders. As anniversaries, holidays, and other special occasions occur don't berate yourself for being sad. It may be helpful to consider temporarily changing or suspending family traditions that serve as painful reminders of happier times.

Allow yourself time to heal. You don't have to rush yourself. Losing someone to suicide is a deep wound. The healing will take place at its own pace. Don't allow the expectations of others to rush you through the process.

There will be setbacks. Some days will be better than others. There will be times when you will think the grief process is over. Suddenly, it appears again. This may occur years after the suicide. Healing doesn't often happen in accordance with a recipe.

During the process, reach out to family, friends, and spiritual leaders for consolation. Don't isolate yourself. Surround yourself with people who are willing to listen when you need to talk.

Grieve in your own way and in your own time. Consider a support group for families affected by suicide. Sharing your story with others who are experiencing the same type of grief may help as you go through the process. It may aid in getting oil to the wound.

But every man is tempted, when he is drawn away of his own lust, and enticed.
James 1:14 NIV

There is another type of suicide that may be more painful. With this type of suicide, the victim survives. There is seemingly no end to their pain and suffering. The victim lives with the idea that others have watched them die. The wound is self-inflicted. It is not a mere hurt; it is a wound. This is spiritual suicide.

While physical suicide is disturbing and confusing, spiritual suicide is even more so. Unlike physical life, spiritual life comes by choice. One is made alive spiritually by obeying the gospel of Christ. This is an individual choice. No one can make this choice for you. Just as it is with physical suicide, thousands of people commit spiritual suicide each year.

Then, after desire has conceived, it gives birth to sin; and sin, when it is full-grown, gives birth to death.
James 1:15 NIV

Shame is often at the core of spiritual suicide. Nearly everyone in our culture has experienced shame at one time or another. Many of us experience shame as a formidable foe ready to rear its head without warning. Shame can result in a disconnection from God, self, other people, society, and the church. When experienced on a regular basis, this disconnection leads to spiritual suicide, the death of the spirit.

Spiritual suicide can be recognized once

we know what to look for. On an individual basis, spiritual suicide manifests itself through feelings of hopelessness. There is no one else to blame for depth of the pain. It wasn't a planned suicide. The victim never saw it coming. Now, they never see it ending. They were carried away from their relationship with God by their own lust. There is no one else to clean up the aftermath.

While you assume that everyone knows that you died, no one is noticing your pain. You are uncomfortable socializing in the world. Yet, guilt says you no longer belong in the church. There are no comforting words at your funeral. There are no flowers or fancy food dishes. No one is sitting around remembering the good old days. There is no celebration of your life.

It is a lonely place. It is an isolated place. It is place overshadowed by the taint of suicide. If you are committing spiritual suicide, what can you do to stop it? Where can you run? Where can you hide? Who will understand? Is there oil for your wounds?

Start by admitting that you are not

happy. Ask God to restore the joy of your salvation. Turn back to Him with all your heart. Next, ask Him to provide direction for your life. Start planning a strategy to help you become the person you were meant to be. And then, it is my hope that you are finally able to do the work that will bring glory to God.

> In a burst of anger I turned My face away
> for a little while. But with everlasting love
> I will have compassion on you,"
> says the LORD, your Redeemer.
> Isaiah 54:8 NLT

There is one who cares for you. He loves you with an everlasting love. He will not turn His face forever. He will abundantly pardon all your iniquities. He is waiting for you to return to Him. He has purpose for your pain. Won't you allow Him to pour oil into your wounds today?

Wilt Thou

"Dear woman," Jesus said to her, "your faith is great. Your request is granted." And her daughter was instantly healed.
Matthew 15:28 NLT

This woman exercised great faith. She was rewarded by receiving an instant healing. Although she was a Gentile woman, she humbly and persistently pleaded with Jesus to heal her child. She was willing to risk everything to receive the miracle that she needed. This included her life.

In times of trouble, do we have such faith? Are we willing to fall to our knees, putting all thoughts of ourselves and what people think of us aside, begging God to hear our prayers? An even bigger question is, "Do we really believe that God will answer our prayers?" It may be easy to think that we would have had the same faith and response that this woman had.

Just as Jesus tested this Gentile woman's faith before He granted her request, so God often tests our faith. When we are in situations where there seems to be no way out, we come to a place where there is nowhere else to look but up. This is the time for us to fall on our knees, putting all thoughts of ourselves and what people think of us aside. It is a time when we beg God to hear our prayers. He always answers our prayers. Sometimes, the answer is, "Yes." At other times the answer may be, "No." Sometimes, the answer is, "You have to wait!" Maybe this what it takes for us to hear what He's been saying all along!

> You can be sure of this: The LORD set apart
> the godly for Himself. The LORD will
> answer when I call to Him.
> Psalm 4:3 NLT

David knew that God would hear him when he called Him. He was confident that God would answer him. We too can be assured that God listens to our prayers. We can be confident that He will answer when we call Him. Sometimes, we think that God will not hear us. Because we have failed to uphold His standards for holy living, we feel that God is a far off. If we have trusted Christ as our savior, God has forgiven us for our sins. We can be sure that He will listen to us.

When you feel that your prayers are hindered, remember that as a believer Jesus paid the sacrifice for your sin. You have been called for a purpose. You are set apart by God and He loves you. He hears and answers our prayers. His answers may not be the ones that you desire. Look at your problems through the greatness of God's power. Don't look at your problems through your own strength.

Faith is the confidence that what we hope for will actually happen; it gives us assurance about things we cannot see.
Hebrews 11:1 NLT

It is often easy to find ourselves only having faith when we can see a glimpse of what lies ahead. It can be easy to have faith when we see what we are hoping for has become a real possibility. When we can't see what lies ahead, we often become despondent and frustrated. We start working harder, believing that we have to make things happen. We start to put faith in ourselves and not in God. We start to believe that God needs our help. Perhaps, we believe that God needs our help.

Search for the LORD and for His strength; continually seek Him. Remember the wonders He has performed, His miracles, and the rulings He has given.
Psalm 105:4-5 NLT

The psalmist suggested a valuable way to find God. We can find Him in our present troubles when we become familiar with the way He has helped His people in the past. In

searching the Bible, we will discover a loving
God who is waiting for us to find Him.

O LORD my God, in You I have taken refuge;
Save me from all those who pursue me,
and deliver me,
Psalm 7:1 NAS

If God seems far from
you, persist in your quest
to find Him. God rewards
those who sincerely
look for Him. The
Word promises, "I will
be found of thee."
How will you
respond when your
faith is tested? Will
you start putting faith in yourself and start
working harder, or will you run to God? Will
you fall into His arms, rest in His presence,
and allow Him to guide your life? Are you
willing to be as shamelessly persistent as
that Gentile woman on that dusty road?

But the LORD is in His holy Temple; the LORD
still rules from heaven. He watches everyone
closely, examining every person on earth.
Psalm 11:4 NLT

When it seems that the foundations are
shaking in your life and you wish you could

hide, remember that God is still in control. His power is not diminished by any turn of events. Nothing ever happens without His knowledge and His permission. When you feel like running away, run to the rock of your salvation; run to the God who never shakes. He will restore justice and goodness on the earth in His good time.

Let us not give up meeting together, as some are in the habit of doing but let us encourage one another--and all the more as you see the Day approaching.
Hebrews 10:25 NIV

In this life, we will have wounds. These will occur inside and outside of the church. Many of these things happen to shake our faith and cause us to turn away from God. As the attacks increase, we have to contend for faith even harder. There is no perfect church because there are no perfect people.

As we grow and mature, we can recover from our wounds. As wounds heal, we will stop bleeding on others. We will accept God's purpose and plan for our life. As God has poured oil into our wounds, we will be able to pour into others.

"Jesus saith unto him, Wilt thou be made whole? The impotent man answered Him, Sir, I have no

man to put me into the pool. Jesus
saith unto him, Rise and walk.
Immediately the man was made
whole, and walked."
John v. 5:6-9

Have faith in God. He
has a purpose for your life.
He has a purpose for your
wounds. He will answer your
prayers. He is willing to
restore you to wholeness.
He has oil for your wounds.
Wilt thou be made whole?

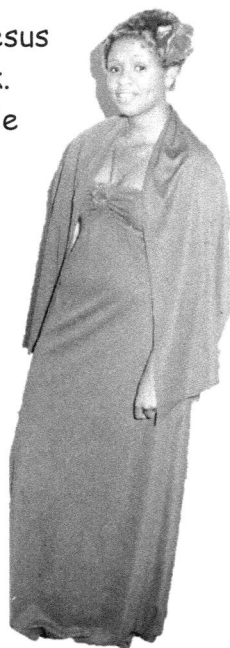

God Made me

**And I will lay sinews upon you, and will
bring up flesh upon you, and cover you
with skin, and put breath in you,
and ye shall live; and ye shall know that
I [am] the LORD.
Ezekiel 37:6**

The pains and wounds in my life have been used by God to make me who I am. When we endure trials in our life, we are faced with a choice. We can allow our trials to make us angry and resentful or we can allow them to make us stronger. When faced with obstacles in my life, I have chosen to grow stronger from them.

A number of years ago, I was interviewed about my first book. Prior to taping the show, my mother and I spent some with the host. The host had just finished reading *A Journey to Hell and Back*. Something about my relationship with my ex-husband, Robert, triggered a negative memory in her life.

Angrily, she said, "I hate Robert! I just hate him!"

Mama interrupted her, "No! No! I love him!"

How could my mother make this statement? It's the truth! While I was still in intensive care, Robert brought food to the hospital for Mama to eat. One person asked her how she was able to eat it, knowing that domestic violence was directly responsible for my plight.

Mama responded, "I am not trying to go to hell! It's by God's grace! I'm not going to let anybody make me hate them!"

Mama maintained a positive attitude throughout my recovery. When one of Mama's friends came to see her, she wanted to encourage Mama. She walked up to Mama with her head hung down.

With a voice of authority, Mama said, "Hold your head up! My child lived!"

Before I was released from the hospital, psychiatrists met with me. Later, they met with Mama. They were concerned about my ability to cope with the trauma. They were also concerned with Mama's ability to cope with the stress of my recovery.

Mama assured them, "It will not be a burden for me! I thank God that He allowed me to be here when my child needs me."

Each of us has good qualities and bad qualities. When people read my first book, they often have negative feelings about Robert. I have many painful memories of that relationship. There are no real memories of a marriage. It is difficult for me to imagine that I did marry him. Today, I consider Robert a friend. There is very little that he wouldn't do for me. My choice to forgive Robert was the right one.

And He said unto me, Son of man, can these
bones live? And I answered,
O Lord GOD, thou knowest.
Ezekiel 37:3

When I was at the point of death, my salvation became more important than revenge. If God was willing to forgive me, I needed to forgive Robert. Anger and bitterness would have delayed my recovery. I allowed God to pour the oil of forgiveness into my wounds.

When I asked Earline about her feelings for Robert, she was reluctant to discuss them. She was there on that near-fatal day. She was four years old at the time. She had no understanding of hate. She didn't fully understand what had happened. Therefore, she did not assign any malice to Robert. Years later, she began to understand why other people were angry with him about that day. She was confused and uncomfortable talking about it.

When I wrote my first book, my family was provided the opportunity to read it prior to publication. Prior to that time, I had never discussed the abuse with anyone other than Mama and my husband, Buck. It was not my desire to breed hatred in my children. Therefore, I didn't discuss this painful information with them. No one else was allowed to discuss it with them.

And it shall come to pass, when your children shall say unto you, What mean ye by this service?
Exodus 12:26

Earline has always loved Robert. After reading the book, Earline would not allow anyone to talk to her in detail about that day. She was uncomfortable when other people wanted to discuss it in detail. She hates the words, burned up. When people discuss the book as entertainment, it is still painful for her. She hates the thought of people being entertained by my pain.

Earline has not processed all of her feelings towards Robert. She does not express anger or resentment towards him. She continues to treat him with respect and love. She remembers him as being a good father figure and treating her as if she were his own child. Earline knows that he has problems. It's odd for her to think about something that she doesn't remember clearly. Robert and Earline have never discussed that day. People who weren't there tried to explain to her the events of that day.

But if ye will not hear it, my soul shall weep in secret places for your pride; and mine eye shall weep sore, and run down with tears, because the LORD'S flock is carried away captive.
Jeremiah 13:17

After being confused about that day for so long, she finds it difficult to assign feelings to it now. For years, she had feelings of guilt. She blamed herself for what happened that day. When the fighting started, I sent her next door to the neighbor's apartment. The neighbors had a big boulder constrictor. She was angry at having to be in the house with the snake.

Instead, I have calmed and quieted myself, like a weaned child who no longer cries for its mother's milk. Yes, like a weaned child is my soul within me.
Psalm 131:2 NLT

Thinking the fighting had ended, she slipped quietly back into the house. After hearing the fighting was ongoing, Earline went back to her room to complete her school-work. She remembers being in her bedroom and seeing me pass by quickly and noticing something burning in the bathroom. Earline decided to see what was happening. She saw the paper burning in the bathroom. It looked like a little fire but she couldn't understand why we didn't put it out. Earline thought about attempting to extinguish the fire. She knew that if you were on fire, you should stop, drop, and roll.

Be strong and courageous. Do not be terrified; do not be discouraged, for the Lord your God will be with you wherever you go.
Joshua 1:9 NIV

After hearing a sound from the bed-room, Earline became scared and ran from the apartment. She decided the fire department needed to be called. She rushed back to the neighbor's apartment. She asked the neighbor to call them. She was terrified that something was wrong inside the bedroom.

The neighbor wouldn't let her out of the house the second time. The neighbor later told her that I would not be able to take care of her and that I was going to the hospital. She asked Earline for a telephone number to contact someone in her family. Initially, she was too nervous to remember the numbers. Eventually, she gave her the number for her grandmother in Columbus, GA.

Somehow, a family member took Earline to the hospital. She wasn't allowed to see me. At some point, police officers interviewed her. When she got older, she blamed herself for Robert not being arrested. She had told the police officer that she saw me throw the paper into the bathroom. She told them it was an accident; she assumed that the house had caught fire.

At the hospital, she saw Robert walk into the room. His hair was white. She thought he had been so scared that his hair turned white or ashes made his hair turn white.

My Aunt Bobbie was angry that Robert was there. Earline remembers that my mother was just scared; she was trying to get my aunt to calm down and focus on what was important, my life. Earline thought it was an accident. My aunt didn't want to hear that. She was convinced that she knew what had happened. On one occasion, she had been on the phone with me when Robert beat me.

Earline didn't see me again until I returned home from the hospital, over three months later. She was surprised that I was so sick. No one had bothered to explain this to her. She assumed that when I came home, I would be well. For most of my life, my family subscribed to a philosophy that children should be seen and not heard. Adult problems weren't discussed with children. Eventually, Mama explained to Earline that I would have to learn how to walk and how to do other things again.

Until Earline read the draft of A Journey to Hell and Back, she harbored feelings of confusion and guilt. She blamed herself for the arguments and not putting the fire out. Because of her feelings of guilt, her other feelings towards Robert were confused. She believes that it was also hard for Robert to deal with what happened that day and that he has unexpressed remorse. Earline feels that his generosity is his way of apologizing. Although he has never stated remorse to her, his continued financial and emotional support indicates to her that he regrets that day. It is her opinion that he regrets the fire, not the abuse.

When she looks at Robert, she sees a man who is broken and who appreciates having a continued opportunity to have his children in his life. She is not blind to his weak-nesses or past mistakes. When thinking back on his mistakes, she is unable to separate them from the man who gave her his last name and unselfishly raised her as his own child. These acts enabled her to hide from her shame at being illegitimate and feeling unwanted by her natural father.

Robert taught Earline how to cook, gave her a love for reading by encouraging her to read one page from the dictionary each day, encouraged her academic success, moved her into her first apartment, visited her when I was in prison, and remained in her life following the divorce from me. She is not blind to his past, his frailty, weakness, and humanity but she also sees his love.

Earline doesn't understand how bad things come from good people. Yet, she understands that sin is the culprit. Without God, a man left to his own devices will do anything. She sees Robert as a man who has been unable to live life on life's terms. When looking back on her own mistakes, it helps her to be more tolerant of others.

There are "friends" who destroy each other but a real friend sticks closer than a brother.
Proverbs 18:24 NLT

After reading the draft of the book, Joe was angry and bitter. He chose to medicate these feelings. He didn't know with whom he could discuss his wounds. Joe began to feel bitterness and resentment towards all men. He later realized that my mother and I had forgiven Robert. This gave him the desire to want to forgive him, too. Joe says he sees remorse in Robert. He has talked to Joe about that day a couple of times. Once, Robert cried as they discussed that day. Robert denied that he ever hit me.

From the time Joe was a small child, Robert has told him, "Don't be like me! Be better than me!"

Because of my abuse, Joe takes extra care to be charming. He always tries to be a gentleman and considerate. As a child, he made a vow to himself that he would never beat his wife. Most of the women Joe meets have experienced some form of physical, verbal, spiritual, or sexual abuse.

Joe was raised around many women. He has received lots of affection from women in the family, the neighborhood, the church, the schools, and my friends. Joe feels that being raised around so many women makes him highly attentive to their wounds and causes him to spread himself too thin, at times. Because he has met so many women who have been wounded and scorned by men, he feels an obligation to show them that "all men aren't the same." His efforts to go out of his way to be charming are his way of compensating for the damage done by his father.

Many women often assume that Joe's attention, affection, and empathy are synonymous with romantic interest. He flirts with most of the women he meets. This flirtation has little to do with physical appearance; he does not discriminate. He has been a flirt most of his life. My uncle started this habit. As a toddler, my uncle would take Joe with him when he was on the prowl for women.

Uncle T said, "I take him with me to help me catch! When he's walking around, they stop and say, 'Look at him. He's so short and cute.' That's all it takes!"

Joe likes to make all women feel valued. He is overprotective of all the women who he loves. From the time, he was about seven years old, adult women began sharing their personal problems with him. He is a compassionate listener and friend. He has provided sound Biblical advice.

Before reading the draft of my first book, Joe was vaguely aware of how I had been burned. He remembers one day as I was applying the rod of correction, he screamed that he wanted his father. He states that I stopped whipping him and asked him if he knew how I had been burned. All that I said to him was that it was his father's fault. Although he wondered what that meant, he never asked. As a small child, Joe didn't know that I had been burned. He assumed that I was born this way. Over the years, people have tried to tell him what happened. He acted as if it didn't hurt. He chose to hide his wounds.

Now Israel loved Joseph more than all his children, because he was the son of his old age: and he made him a coat of many colors.
Genesis 37:3

Joe has his own way of dealing with his wounds; he doesn't. Joe is the apple of his father's eye. There is no denying this fact. He still refers to him as "his boy." He will give Joe anything that he has in his possession. Robert is extremely proud of his son. They share a very close relationship.

Joe was not raised to hate his father. He has always been present in his life. He has never disciplined him, to do so would bring about my wrath. Joe is also extremely close to his stepfather, Buck. He has never said anything negative about Robert to Joe.

Over the years, Joe has heard many negative things about his father. He didn't hear them from me. Even after reading A Journey to Hell and Back, he has never discussed any negative emotions concerning Robert. He found oil for his wounds in the Word of God.

Joe doesn't like to discuss negative things about anybody. This includes negative things about strangers. Sometimes, I think that he hates to hear that the weather is going to be bad. He prefers to live in a world where there are no pains and wounds. He is very accepting of people and looks beyond their flaws and imperfections. Joe is also very forgiving. He's a compassionate friend. If he is your friend, he will never do you harm. He easily forgives friends who do him wrong.

How much better to get wisdom than gold, to get insight rather than silver!
Proverbs 16:16 NIV

La'Toya, my granddaughter had to come to terms with what happened. She tells it like this:

Until the first book came out, I never knew what happened. A lot was kept from me and initially the first book was, too. When I got the chance, I snuck and read it. I never knew that my grandma had been burned. At that age, I assumed that it was her skin and that everybody was different. I was around eight when the first book came out. At that age, I didn't know what skin grafts were.

All my life, he'd been my grandfather. He was so nice to us; he gave us food and money. He lived down the street from my great grandma. We would walk down the street to visit him.

When I finally read the book, I was in shock. It was really hard to believe that he could have done anything that heinous. As long as I've known him, he's been somewhat weak. And honestly, I believed my grandma could take him. I never knew the old strong him. I was confused for a while after I found out but then nothing changed for anyone else. When you're young, you just follow the cues of the adults in your family.

As an adult, whenever I see them interact, there is the thought in the back of my head. It's saying, 'Wow! I don't know if I could do it. They act as if nothing happened. I wonder if he even remembers.' Then, they start cracking jokes and he proposes to her.

Husbands, love your wives, and
be not bitter against them.
Colossians 3:19

People often remark that I was a blessing to my husband, Buck. They give me credit for him being who he is today. While it is true that God used me to bring about change in his life, there is a flip side. God used Buck to bring about healing in my life. When I met him, I was still trapped in a cycle of fear. The domestic violence had left me wounded physically and emotionally. When Buck became a part of my life, the fear subsided. I don't fear Robert or anyone else.

Buck's unconditional love also brought healing to my life in other areas. While I am a good thing and a virtuous woman, I am not a perfect woman. On many occasions, I deliberately provoked him. It was not because I meant him evil; I was trying to force change. Rather than becoming angry with me, he continued to love me unconditionally. Buck pushed me to excel in many areas. Because God used him to make me, he shares in all my accomplishment.

Then I passed by and saw you kicking about in your blood, and as you lay there in your blood I said to you, "Live!"
Ezekiel 16:6

When people looked at me lying in that hospital bed, my recovery was doubtful. With every new accomplishment in my life, I stand in awe of God. With each graduation, with each book, and with each positive act, I look up to God and ask, "You did that?! Wow!"

And the fruit of righteousness is sown in peace of them that make peace.
James 3:18

Another painful event happened to me. A young woman who didn't know me at all was discussing me with a group of people who should have known me relatively well. My education and I offended her. I was found guilty of this offense.

In an open group, it was said, "She thinks she knows everything! She thinks she has more education than anybody else does. She is always commenting behind someone else."

Several people in the room should have been able to bring about peace. Evangelist Elena was new to the group and the members were overly concerned about her feelings. When news of the discussion came back to me, I was upset and hurt. These feelings were not directed at this woman but at those who should have known my character.

For the kingdom of God is not a matter of eating and drinking but of righteousness, peace and joy

in the Holy Spirit, because anyone who serves Christ in this way is pleasing to God and approved by men. Let us therefore make every effort to do what leads to peace and to mutual edification.
Romans 14:17-19 NIV

When I attempted to make peace with Evangelist Welena, it made matters worse. Because others appeared to agree with her opinion, she was convinced that she was right. Rather than diffusing the situation, they caused the matter to escalate. When I realized how angry she was, I asked for someone else to mediate. Instead of helping the situation, this made matters even worse.

Several people were present at the informal meeting. Accusations from a woman who barely knew me didn't hurt. Evangelist Welena was loud and boisterous; that's not what hurt. She had made an assumption about me without complete facts.

The Bible warns us about judging anything before its time. We often make assumptions about people based on our first impression. In every organization, there is a Person considered a troublemaker. The person considered the troublemaker spoke up for me. Sometimes, the troublemaker is just the person who dares to stand up against wrong. Jesus was considered a troublemaker by some religious rulers.

Our impressions are often flawed by something within us. Jealousy, envy, and insecurity can cloud anyone's perception. It is never possible to know fully what another person is thinking or feeling. However, we often assume the person is thinking or feeling exactly the way we would feel in that same situation.

> Therefore you have no excuse, every one of you
> who passes judgment, for in that which you judge
> another, you condemn yourself; for you who judge
> practice the same things.
>
> Romans 2:1

With her finger waving in my face, Evangelist Welena screamed, "You think you have more education than anyone else! You are always bragging on your education! I have a master's degree in counseling! I have two years of seminary!"

> I'm ashamed to say that we've been too "weak" to
> do that! But whatever they dare to boast about—
> I'm talking like a fool again—
> I dare to boast about it, too.
>
> 2 Corinthians 11:21 NLT

Evangelist Welena's words proved that

she didn't know me. She had not heard me brag about my education; she didn't even know how much education I had. By the grace of God, I have a master's and a doctorate degree in counseling. Additionally, I have attended at least five seminaries for a combined total of over ten years in seminary training. On the back of each of my books, it states that my GED is my proudest degree.

So I spoke the message as He commanded me, and breath came into their bodies. They all came to life and stood up on their feet—a great army.
Ezekiel 37:10 NLT

One of the cornerstones of my ministry is encouraging people to pursue higher education. No matter how old you are, you can begin again; I did. Education is not some-thing that I recently began promoting. I have taught work-readiness classes and job training classes. I have tutored others to prepare them for high school graduation and the GED test. I have also volunteered to speak at numerous community-based organizations to encourage people to pick up the pieces of their life and start over. On more than one occasion, I have driven hundreds of miles to speak at a GED graduation inside of a prison.

Evangelist Welena's didn't know any of this about me. She destroyed my first impression of her; but she didn't wound me. Until that day, I viewed her as a mature Christian whom I respected. I didn't know her either.

And one shall say unto him, What are these wounds in thine hands? Then he shall answer, Those with which I was wounded in the house of my friends.
Zechariah 13:6

There was another woman present. Until that day, I thought we were friends. Apis had recently gone through a major personal tragedy. Without any consideration for my health, or myself I had walked through the valley of the shadow of death and the valley of death with her. As we stood there, she told me that she hated me. This was the wound.

Without mincing words, Apis said, "I hate you! Don't you understand?! I can't stand you! I tell you all the time! You just laugh! It's not funny! I'm serious! I can't stand you!"

Truthfully, Apis had said this to me on numerous occasions inside the church. Each time, I laughed. It was difficult for me to imagine any professing Christian being this cruel. Her behaviors had also sent an unclear message to me. While stating that she hated me, Apis talked to me about her personal and private information.

Apis shared with me how others had shunned her, told her personal business, and discussed the crisis in her life without compassion. I had encouraged many others with the same problem in the past.

The spirit of a man will sustain his infirmity; but a wounded spirit who can bear?
Proverbs 18:14

Later, when her husband died, I wrote his obituary, made handkerchiefs for her to place over her lap, edited and prepared a picture of him for display at the funeral, and offered continued support to her through her personal crisis, which was ongoing following his death. I am not telling the things that I did for Apis for vainglory but to help clarify why I was shocked about the nature of her feelings towards me. I could not understand how you could allow someone you hate into your intimate personal circle.

Apis further stated that she did not care for me to sit by her. Just a few months before, she had sat in my car next to me. Apis called me to drive her to the hospital when her husband passed. That wasn't the first time that I accompanied her to the hospital. After his passing, I sat next to her assisting her with funeral arrangements. From her husband's hospital room, I called immediate family and friends to notify them of his death. While waiting for the funeral home to arrive to pick up his body, I stayed in the room with her and his corpse.

A merry heart doeth good like a medicine: but a broken spirit drieth the bones.
Proverbs 17:22

It was perhaps the most hateful thing that any professing Christian had ever said to me at that time. As Apis yelled her insults at me, tears streamed down my face; I was wounded but not beyond repair. God has given me a gift of laughter. In the face of almost any pain, I can laugh. This day, the gift didn't operate. For several days, it didn't operate.

And Moses said unto the people, Fear ye not, stand still, and see the salvation of the LORD, which He will shew to you today: for the Egyptians whom ye have seen today, ye shall see them again no more forever.
Exodus 14:13

The entire event was cruel and heartless. It was so cruel that I will not repeat it in its entirety. On more than one occasion, I had come to her defense when others spoke about negative things Apis had done. I a-lowed this woman space in my life. The very words spoken from her mouth enabled me to delete her from my life. It came to a point where she was able to walk past me and I didn't have to avoid looking at her; she no longer existed in my world. There is no hate or animosity towards her.

Apis later came to me. While hugging me, she said, "Let's just forget about what happened and go on." It was kind of an apology. I decided to accept it as one.

Ironically, the person labeled as a troublemaker poured oil into my wound. She never told me anything that was said about me. Recognizing my pain, she walked over to me and hugged me.

She said very gently, "I love you and I appreciate you so much!"

Why was Apis angry with me? She was angry with me. She was angry before her husband died. After his death, she still had unresolved issues of angry with him. She needed to take her anger out on someone; I was available.

Sometimes, what people hate about you is also, what they love about you in their time of need. People may hate that you have a domineering personality; when someone takes advantage of them, they depend on this person to defend them. People may hate that your finances are stable; when they have a financial crisis, they seek your help.

Shortly after Mama gave her life to Christ, an elderly Christian woman asked her, "Baby have you learned that you can't please everybody yet?"

After I was burned, I was hospitalized for over three months in Atlanta, GA. Mama was living in Columbus, GA. Every Friday, Mama rode the bus to Atlanta to see me in the hospital. Each Sunday night, she rode the bus back to Columbus. Mama attended Bible study each week but missed Sunday morning services. During her visits at the hospital, we continuously watched Christian programs on television.

One of Mama's friends warned her, "Miss Russell, don't forget about God because your daughter is in the hospital!"

Mama was deeply concerned about her comments. Mama knew a wise elderly Christian woman. Miss Bailey could be trusted to tell her the truth. She decided to ask Miss Bailey. She explained her concerns.

Miss Bailey sternly replied, "Miss Russell, if you didn't go see your daughter in the hospital, you wouldn't even be a mother, let alone a Christian.

After I was released from the hospital, Mama had a second conversation with her friend. Her friend said, "Miss Russell, you really stuck by your daughter when she was in the hospital!"

Inwardly Mama said, "If I had listened to you, I wouldn't have."

"And the LORD will continually guide you, And satisfy your desire in scorched places, And give strength to your bones; And you will be like a watered garden, And like a spring of water whose waters do not fail.
Isaiah 58:11 NAS

One day, I was attempting to sing *God Made Me.* Singing is not a gift that God gave me. As a group of children passed by me, the youngest one started singing the song correctly. When I asked her to continue, they all sang for me.

When I received my doctorate, I decided that I would only tell my immediate family. For years, I had been a master at pretending to be educationally challenged. This was done in an effort to fit in somewhere that I didn't fit. Even now, I am often tempted to minimize my education. God convicted me of this behavior. When a high school dropout with a GED earns a doctorate, God gets the glory.

When I was asked to apologize to Evangelist Welena, I did so as a courtesy to the leaders. It was also out of my respect for them. It was not from a heartfelt conviction. For the things that were said to me, there was never an apology; I didn't expect one.

In my life, I have apologized for a wrong or perceived wrong precipitated by me. They came from my heart. This apology was a farce; I could never apologize for who God made me to be. You may not like who I am; you have that right. If I have to be a fake for you to like me, you still don't like me. The price that was paid for me was too great for a fake. The wounds were too deep. The cost of my education... The price that Jesus paid for my redemption, it was an unspeakable gift.

Looking at my dry bones, there was nothing that said I would live or breathe again. God literally caused my flesh to come back. He blew the breath back into my lungs. He gave me another chance at life. Yes! He made me who I am! For what God has done, I will not apologize. He will get the glory that He deserves. Man couldn't do what God did for me. God made me who I am! From the crown of my head to the soul of feet, He poured oil on me to heal my wounds.

.

Other Titles
By
Dr. Charlotte Russell Johnson

ISBN 0974189308

ISBN 0974189316

ISBN 0974189324

ISBN 0974189332

ISBN 0974179340

ISBN 0974189359

ISBN 0974189369

ISBN 0974189375

ISBN 0974189383

Reaching Beyond, Inc.
www.charlotterjohnson.com

Helping hurting humanity to reach beyond the barriers in their life, one barrier at a time.

ORDER FORM

Know someone else in crisis, or in need of encouragement order additional copies of this book to sow seeds of healing grace.

Postal Orders:

Reaching Beyond, Inc.
P. O. Box 12364
Columbus, GA 31917-2364
(706) 573-5942
Email us at: admin@charlotterjohnson.com
Please send the following book(s).

Qty.	Title	
_____	*A Journey to Hell and Back*	$14.95 each
_____	*The Flip Side*	$15.95 each
_____	*Daddy's Hugs*	$12.95 each
_____	*Grace Under Fire*	$14.95 each
_____	*Mama May I*	$14.95 each
_____	*Mama's Pearls*	$14.95 each
_____	*Breaking the Curse*	$14.95 each
_____	*Kissin' Hell Goodbye*	$14.95 each
_____	*Oil for the Wounded*	$14.95 each

Sales tax:
  Please add 7% for books shipped to GA addresses.
Shipment:
  Book rate $3.50 for the first book and $1.75 for each additional book.
              Also available at www.charlotterjohnson.com

.

www.ingramcontent.com/pod-product-compliance
Lightning Source LLC
La Vergne TN
LVHW051504080426
835509LV00017B/1918